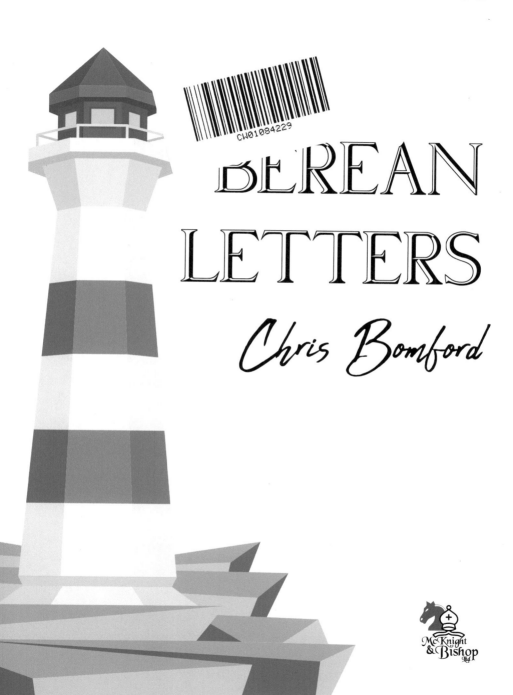

CW01084229

BEREAN

LETTERS

Chris Bomford

McKnight
& Bishop
Ltd

ABOUT THE PUBLISHER

McKnight & Bishop are always on the lookout for new authors and ideas for new books. If you write or if you have an idea for a book, please email:

info@mcknightbishop.com

Some things we love are undiscovered authors, open-source software, Creative Commons, crowd-funding, Amazon/Kindle, faith, social networking, laughter and new ideas.
Visit us at **www.mcknightbishop.com**

Copyright © Chris Bomford 2021

The rights of Chris Bomford to be identified as the Author of this Work has been asserted by him in accordance with Section 77 of the Copyright, Designs and Patents Act 1988.

The views expressed in this work are solely those of the author and do not necessarily reflect the views of the publisher, and the publisher hereby disclaims any responsibility for them.

All Scripture quotations, unless otherwise indicated, are taken from the Holy Bible, New International Version®, NIV®. Copyright ©1973, 1978, 1984, 2011 by Biblica, Inc.™ Used by permission of Zondervan. All rights reserved worldwide. www.zondervan.com The "NIV" and "New International Version" are trademarks registered in the United States Patent and Trademark Office by Biblica, Inc.™

ISBN 978-1-905691-72-2

A CIP catalogue record for this book is available from the British Library.

First published in 2022 by McKnight & Bishop Inspire, an imprint of:

McKnight & Bishop Ltd
2 Charles Street, Thurcroft, Rotherham, South Yorkshire, S66 9HQ
http://www.mcknightbishop.com | info@mcknightbishop.com

This book has been typeset in Garamond, VIA APPIA, Gill Sans MT, Abuget and Viner Hand ITC.

Printed and bound in Great Britain by
Mixam UK Ltd. 6 Hercules Way, Watford, Hertfordshire WD25 7GS

DEDICATION

I think back to when I became a Christian in the late 1980s and had little real understanding of the Christian faith. My dear wife Heather had been saved several years earlier and was already attending a local village church. I am so grateful for her prayers as she waited for me to see the light and that we have been able to share our Christian lives together ever since.

I want to dedicate this book to all the people who have helped me on my Christian journey. That little Essex village fellowship where it began. The Bible teachers at Plumbline Ministries who ran the Colchester Bible School. The faithful men and women who opened my spiritual eyes over the last 30 or more years. I think of Derek Prince, Colin Urquhart, Andrew Wommack, Joseph Prince and many others. They all had an important part to play in challenging my misconceptions and leading me into the truth of Kingdom life. I will want to track them down in heaven to thank them!

But my biggest thanks are to my Saviour, the Lord Jesus Christ. Every good thing in my life is because of Him and the glory goes to Him.

Chris Bomford

December 2021

CONTENTS

WHY BEREAN?
AN INTRODUCTION

Every one of us grows up in a culture. It is the prevailing environment we are born into and grow up in, whether it is family, the local community, nation or area of the planet we live in. Even in church there are denominational cultures that shape our thinking, behaviour, attitudes and reactions. This is not always obvious to us until we are faced with something that challenges our system of belief. Do we instinctively reject or will we honestly evaluate it to see whether there is any truth in what we have bumped into? Church history is littered with such events, just ask Martin Luther how his revelation of justification by faith alone went down with the established church authorities! What we see is that there is a cultural inertia in church which resists change and can rob us of increasing revelations of God's goodness to us expressed in His Son Jesus Christ. I am not suggesting we take in any or every idea that floats by us as we are urged to weigh and test everything to see whether it lines up with God's word. There is a very good biblical illustration of what I am talking about.

When Paul and Silas went to Macedonia to preach the gospel they visited Thessalonica. As was his custom Paul went to the synagogue and reasoned with them that Jesus was their Messiah. Some were persuaded but other Jews became so angry and stirred up so much opposition that Paul and Silas had to leave town. The prevailing Jewish culture had been challenged and they weren't willing to honestly consider the truth of what Paul was preaching. Now he arrives at Berea and again goes to the synagogue but this time it is different. The book of Acts records: *'Now the Bereans were of more noble character than the Thessalonians, for they received the message with great eagerness and examined the Scriptures every day to see if what Paul said was true.' (Acts 17 v 13).* What an inspiration and challenge for us to be like the Bereans. Because of their willingness to check it out they didn't miss out on God's best for them.

Over the years as I have read the Bible, listened to Bible teaching and preaching I have often been challenged to evaluate my beliefs. I am grateful to those who have done this and helped me to ditch wrong understanding of Bible truths. They have been used to liberate me from unnecessary angst over my relationship with God. I am considerably freer now than I was in the beginning and I know there is more to come as I explore the amazing grace of our Lord Jesus Christ. It is with this spirit that I want to live and why I have felt inspired to write these Berean Letters. The subjects I talk about are those I have puzzled over and know that others have struggled with. My desire is that the Holy Spirit will use them to help others to fully enter into the freedom that is ours in Jesus Christ. As Paul himself wrote *'It is for freedom that Christ has set us free. Stand firm, then, and do not let yourselves be burdened again by a yoke of slavery' (Galatians 5 v 1)*. Amen!

Berean Chris

CHAPTER 1:

THE GREAT OBEDIENCE

J esus made it clear, He only said what the Father told Him to say and He only did what the Father did. In other words He was perfectly obedient to God the Father. There is a passage in the gospels that reveals this obedience and it is when He was led into the wilderness by the Holy Spirit fasting for forty days before being tempted by Satan.

It is a well known event in Jesus life and contains a profound truth about how Jesus reversed the disobedience of man in the Garden of Eden. We can see how Jesus resisted the temptations to misuse His power, test His Father's protection and to worship Satan and own the world. Jesus obedience to the Father's plan to redeem mankind thwarted Satan's plan to derail His rescue mission. After forty days of fasting Jesus was hungry and had the power to change stones into food but He knew His strength didn't come from bread alone but from God's word. Then Satan led Jesus to stand on the highest point of the temple in Jerusalem tempting Him to jump off to test His Father's promise to send angels to keep Him from harm. The Father would have, but it would have been a submission to Satan and a deviation from the Father's will for Him. Finally Jesus was tempted with complete ownership of all the kingdoms of the world if He would give Satan what he craved most of all, worship. Jesus sums it all up by quoting from Deuteronomy: *'Worship the Lord your God, and serve Him only'*. Underlining His perfect obedience to God the Father's will for Him. That is the first level of meaning we see in this event.

But there is a parallel here to what went wrong in the Garden of Eden. In the wilderness Jesus refused to turn stones into bread. In Eden the serpent, who is the agent of Satan, tempts Eve and Adam (yes, he was also there) to eat from the tree of the knowledge of good and evil but they disobeyed God's command and ate. It wasn't the magnitude of this disobedience that mattered but what it released into man's spirit, a natural tendency to disobey when we don't like what we are told to do! When Jesus was on the top of the temple He refused to test God's protection to keep Him from dying if He jumped off. In the Garden the serpent contradicts God by saying they wouldn't die if they eat the forbidden fruit. In the wilderness Jesus refused the offer to rule the world on Satan's terms but in the Garden Adam and Eve believed the lie that by eating the fruit they would be like God, which is they could rule over their own world without reference to their Creator. The whole of mankind has suffered the consequence of their disobedience throughout human history as people fight to have what they want and do what they want. What Jesus did in the wilderness was more than just resist Satan's efforts to derail Jesus' ministry. It was essential to reverse the disobedience in the Garden of Eden that unleashed sin and its consequences into the world.

The apostle Paul summed it up in the book of Romans: *'For just as through the disobedience of the one man the many were made sinners, so also through the obedience of the one man the many will be made righteous' (5 v 19)*. Jesus obedience in the wilderness cancelled out the disobedience in the Garden of Eden. Wonderful! When we believe in Jesus as our Lord and Saviour we are put in the Obedient One. His obedience becomes our obedience to allow us to stand righteous before Almighty God without fear of punishment. Jesus has taken care of everything for us!

CHAPTER 2:
THE CONFUSION
OF CONFESSION

I n the Letter to the Hebrews it tells us that because of the sacrifice of Jesus and His blood that wipes away all our sin we have confidence to be in God's presence *'having our hearts sprinkled to cleanse us from a guilty conscience' (10 v 22)*. At the very least this encourages us to be more aware of the grace that is ours in Christ than sins we have committed or are committing. Another way to put it is living with a forgiven mentality (also see Romans 8 v 1).

But there are doctrines embraced by the church that contradict this and say it is unrealistic as we always need to be aware of our sins and keep confessing and admitting them to God. Even to the point that this is necessary to stay in fellowship with Him as under the Old Covenant of the Law. Sadly this idea produces doubt and uncertainty about the security of our salvation. This can become a crippling fear if we are not sure we have confessed everything or we think there could be sins we are not aware of. This is not what God wants and it is not recognising the complete and final victory over sin and death won by Christ on the cross to set us free from guilt and fear. There is a verse that the church predominantly uses to justify repeated confessions. It is *'If we confess our sins, he is faithful and just and will forgive us our sins and purify us from all unrighteousness' (1 John 1 v 9)*. On the face of it that would seem to back up the keep-confessing-sins doctrine. However we need to see the context and why John wrote this and to whom.

1 John is a corrective letter to combat dangerous ideas creeping into the church and to bring it back to God's purpose to be full of His light and love (this is a repetitive theme in his letter). In this first chapter he is confronting three particular errors. The first is that a holy God couldn't

possibly inhabit sinful human flesh meaning that Jesus was not really human. This would presumably mean that Jesus was only a spiritual being. This is why John says *'we have seen with our eyes … our hands have touched … the Word of life' (v 1)*. John refutes this because if Jesus was not 100% human (as well as 100% God) He couldn't have legitimately taken our place and there would be no salvation. John was well qualified to say this as he had travelled with, eat with and lived with Jesus for over three years. The second challenge is to the idea that fellowship with God is based on what we know and that what we do in the body doesn't matter too much. This would give a licence to sin without consequence. This is why John says *'If we claim to have fellowship with him yet walk in the darkness, we lie and do not live by the truth' (v6)*. John is making the point that if Jesus truly was their Saviour and Lord, they wouldn't live like that. The last error he confronts is the one that leads into verse 9. This is the argument that man is not sinful which provokes John to write *'If we claim to be without sin, we deceive ourselves and the truth is not in us' (v8)* and *'we make him out to be a liar' (v10)*. This is why verse 9 was written as it is addressed to people who think they have no sin which is why John says the first thing they have to do is admit they are sinners and in need of salvation. Then when they accept Christ as Saviour they will receive the forgiveness of sins freely offered to them. Salvation is based on the truth that we are all sinners from birth. It can therefore be seen that chapter 1 of John's letter is not primarily addressed to believing Christians but to those on the periphery of the church which is maybe who he refers to later saying they didn't really belong to them but left (see 2 v 19). This all adds up to mean it is incorrect to apply 1 John 1 v 9 to believers in isolation to its true context!

So what is the true place of confession for believers? Christians are capable of sinning like anyone else. But as believers in Christ we have received forgiveness for our sins past, present and future through His once and for all time sacrifice on the cross (see Hebrews 10 v 12). So when we do sin we do not need a fresh sacrifice as in the Old Testament but we can remember the finished work of the cross. In John's letter he picks this up in chapter 2 writing *'But if anyone does sin, we have one who speaks to the Father in our defence – Jesus Christ, the Righteous One. He is the atoning sacrifice for our sins, and not only for ours but also for the sins of the whole world' (2 v 1 – 2).* Forgiveness has already been provided and when we believe in Jesus as our Saviour and continue to believe in Him we are living forgiven! We must avoid the trap of believing that our confession of sins is what keeps us right with God because it doesn't. It is our faith in 'the atoning sacrifice' of Jesus and nothing else that keeps us forgiven and righteous in God's eyes.

This letter is not an argument for not confessing but rather a case of admitting our sins when we are pulled up by the Holy Spirit and immediately thanking Jesus for the victory of the cross. God's plan for us is to live free from guilt and condemnation and He has made that possible through the sacrifice of His own Son Jesus Christ. When we live in grace consciousness we glorify the Saviour!

CHAPTER 3:

WHAT IS REPENTANCE?

I n my early Christian life I ended up with a wrong understanding about repentance. This was possibly because I heard other more experienced believers saying things like 'our nation must repent of its sins otherwise ...' and there seemed to be an inexhaustible list of sins that needed to be dealt with! I equated repentance with a sackcloth and ashes approach to a stern Father God who was more interested in me coming clean than an intimate relationship with Him. But now I know different and I suspect others also need to be liberated from a misunderstanding about repentance and crucially how it figures in our gospel message to the world. Repentance is not a big stick to make people submit to God!

The word repentance is translated from a Greek word that simply means a change of mind. It is clear that this is a decision to think differently and is not an emotion. Emotions may occur at a repentant moment but they are a result not the repentance itself. Furthermore if repentance has really happened then there will be a change of thinking and direction in our lives. It also reveals that repentance happens when we get a revelation of truth that challenges our previous mind set. Perhaps people don't recognise that if we are listening to a preacher who brings us a revelation that changes the way we thought before we have repented. In one sense the Christian life is continuous repentance as we respond to increasing revelation of God's love and grace shown to us through Jesus Christ.

Another point to clarify is remorse is not repentance. The classic example of this is Esau who sold his birthright and the firstborn blessing to his younger brother for a meal when hungry. In the letter to the Hebrews it says: *'He could bring about no change of mind, though he sought the blessing with tears'* *(12 v 17)*. Esau was very sorrowful but it was for what he lost not for the sin of despising his birthright (a big deal in that culture). His lack of true repentance can be seen in the grudge he held against Jacob. It is sobering to realise that if Esau had not despised his birthright he would have been in the lineage of Jesus.

So how does repentance fit into our message to the world today? The Bible records that John the Baptist as the last of the Old Testament prophets preached a message of repentance from sins. He was speaking to Jews under the Law of Moses telling them to stop sinning and get right with God. John the Baptist knew that when he had fulfilled his purpose of preparing the way for the Messiah he would retire from the scene. That handover came when he baptised Jesus in the Jordan. Then Jesus begins His ministry with the words *'The time has come. The Kingdom of God is near. Repent and believe the good news!' (Mark 1 v 15)*. Now here is the shift, signalling a change of covenant from Law keeping to grace. Jesus is saying change you're thinking to believe in Me, I am the good news, I will fulfil the Law for you! Now see the contrast between two sermons that Peter preached. The first is at Pentecost when he tells the assembled Jews that Jesus was and is their Messiah and that they had crucified Him. Shocked and convicted they cry out as to what should they do to which Peter replies *'Repent and be baptised, every one of you, in the name of Jesus Christ for the forgiveness of your sins' (Acts 2 v 38)*. If they will change their minds about Jesus, accept Him as their Messiah, get baptised (a sign of true repentance) their sins will be forgiven. This continues to be the message to the people of Israel today: Change your minds, your Messiah has come, He is Jesus, accept Him and receive God's forgiveness.

But what about us who are not Jews. Now consider the sermon Peter preached to Cornelius a Roman centurion. He is now speaking to people who are not under the Law of Moses who would be free of the strict demands of the Jewish religious system. Those whose mindsets would not be coloured by the idea that God only demands complete obedience from man. His whole sermon is recorded for our benefit and in it Peter does not once use the word repent. Peter describes to his audience how God sent His Son Jesus into the world and by the power of the Holy Spirit went around doing good to all. He recounts how he witnessed all this and His death and resurrection which was all in accordance with the prophets. Peter only gets as far as saying *'everyone who believes in him receives forgiveness of sins through his name' (Acts 10 v 43)* when the Holy Spirit interrupts him by falling on all who heard the message. Then they were all baptised showing that they had truly repented, all without the exhortation to repent! They had a revelation of the truth of Jesus as Saviour of the world that convinced them to trust in Him. This should inform our approach to preaching the gospel.

There is a verse that is often overlooked in the letter to the Romans which says: *'God's kindness leads you towards repentance' (2 v 4)*. That is wonderfully radical and is what happened at the house of Cornelius. The wonderful kindness of God expressed in Jesus was revealed through Peter causing them all to change their minds and embrace the Saviour. This should be the basis of our gospel to our Gentile world. We should not be demanding repentance but proclaiming the good news of salvation in Jesus Christ. That good news of God's kindness will bring people to repent and when they get baptised we will know it is for real!

CHAPTER 4:

THE GREAT CHANGEOVER

At the last supper Jesus said to His disciples *'This cup is the new covenant in my blood, which is poured out for you'* (*Luke 22 v 20*). This is celebrated as part of communion which is taken widely throughout the church. We thank Him for His body being broken for us so that we can be made whole and the shedding of His blood for the forgiveness of our sins. But there is also His statement that this a new covenant. What is the implication of this? Is this an additional covenant or one that replaces an existing agreement between God and man? Jesus is speaking to Jews under the Law of Moses which is a covenant of law keeping (if man obeys God's rules He will bless, if they disobey they will suffer curse). In the letter to the Hebrews we find this clarification: *'By calling this covenant "new", he has made the first one obsolete; and what is obsolete and ageing will soon disappear' (8 v 13)*. This explains that the new covenant is not additional but replaces the old. This also makes it clear that there is no mixing of old and new so it is either one or the other!

This question caused a lot of heat in the early church and is perhaps one reason why the letter to the Hebrews was written. Its main thrust was to show that Jesus was God's ultimate revelation to man and superior to Moses by bringing in a new and better covenant. That was a big discussion in itself but when Gentiles started getting saved it raised a new debate that has big implications for us! The issue was should non-Jews have to obey the Law of Moses with all its requirements and rituals including circumcision. This led to the church council meeting at Jerusalem recorded in Acts 15. After much debate the leaders concluded that there was no requirement for Gentiles to obey the Law of Moses but only required them to steer clear of anything connected with idolatry, meat with blood in it and sexual immorality. This would seem to settle the issue and that Gentiles are free from the onerous demands of the Law of Moses.

However there is one outstanding question. While Gentiles do not have to obey all the ritual demands of the Law of Moses what about the requirement to keep the Ten Commandments? The crucial point is are they part of the Law of Moses or a separate code for all to obey to be right with God? They are all part of the Law of Moses given at the same time to the same group of people, the Israelites. In referring to the Law Paul made a startling statement in his second letter to the Corinthians: '... *the ministry that brought death which was engraved in letters on stones' (3 v 7)*. Paul here is referring to the Ten Commandments which were engraved on stone tablets and he describes them as a ministry of death. To better understand this we need to realise the purpose the Law of Moses was given and in his letter to the Galatians chapter 3 he gives us insight. He says *'What, then, was the purpose of the law? It was added because of transgressions ...' (v 19)* meaning that the law was a restraint to limit sin. All laws throughout the world are put in place to restrain unlawful behaviour e.g. speed limits. Even more surprising is his statement *'For if a law had been given that could impart life, then righteousness would certainly have come by the law' (v 21)*. He explains that rule keeping (of any kind) cannot make you righteous and as shown above that includes the Ten Commandments! So what on earth was the law for? Paul writes again *'So the law was put in charge to lead us to Christ that we might be justified by faith. Now that faith has come, we are no longer under the supervision of the law' (v 24 – 25)*. Wonderful, we no longer have to keep laws or rules to be justified before God. We are righteous by faith in Christ! What the Law of Moses did was to flush out our inability to live righteously by law keeping and to bring us to a point of desperation where we saw the need for someone to rescue us from our guilt. In case anyone thought just going through the motions would get them by with God see Jesus' Sermon on the Mount. He said if you get angry with someone that is equivalent to murder and if a man lusts after someone else's wife that equates to adultery. Jesus raises the bar to not just outward obedience but extends to what goes on inside us!

At this point there will be the major objection to all this freedom from rule keeping. If we do not have rules (usually dressed up as guidelines for living) they will be unrestrained in what they do. On the face of it that seems logical as you put rules in place to keep people on the straight and narrow. Interesting to note that all societies end up putting more and more laws in place as people find more ways to be disobedient. What is the Bible's answer to this conundrum? Paul wrote to Titus who had been left to pastor the church in Crete which it seems was a challenging gig with all sorts of moral issues to sort out. But see his advice to Titus *'For the grace of God that brings salvation has appeared to all men. It teaches us to say "No" to ungodliness and worldly passions, and to live self-controlled, upright and godly lives in this present age ...' (Titus 2 v 11 – 12)*. So here is the answer to holy living, not law keeping but having a true revelation of the grace of God shown to us in Jesus Christ. We are saved by grace and we continue by living by grace. To put it in a nutshell if you love Jesus and have a true revelation of His grace you will live holy without realising it!

This is the great changeover. We have received a covenant of grace where the undeserved favour and blessing of God is released to us simply by believing in Jesus as our Lord and Saviour. We are not under any law as a means of getting right with God. And incidentally Gentiles never were under the Law of Moses. We are justified by faith alone and Christ's perfect righteousness is gifted to us so that we can agree with Paul who said we are the righteousness of God in Christ Jesus (see 2 Corinthians 5 v 21).

CHAPTER 5:

SAVE THE PLANET?

There is no doubt that mankind's activity has affected the planet. We are constantly reminded of the damage caused by pollution, destruction of forests, plastics in the sea etc. all a result of our modern world's appetites. With increasing awareness of changes to climate and its potential impact around the world, together with the rise of pressure groups such as Extinction Rebellion what should the church say or do about this. Do we join an appropriate bandwagon to save the planet? Does the Bible have anything to say about all this and if so what?

The Bible does have some surprising things to say about all this and it is not what you hear from many pulpits. Let us start with something Peter wrote: *But the day of the Lord will come like a thief. The heavens will disappear with a roar; the elements will be destroyed by fire, and the earth and everything in it will be burned up' (2 Peter 3 v 10)*. We will not speculate on when that will happen but on the fact that the planet as we know it will dramatically disappear. Also in chapter 21 of the book of Revelation it says that the first heaven, earth and sea will pass away to be replaced by a new heaven and earth. It is clear from the way these two accounts are written that they are to be taken literally and that they not are just allegories for our current planet to be better. This is radical stuff and it represents a challenge to the idea that we can save the planet so it lasts forever. At this point I need to say that I am not suggesting we can live careless and carefree lifestyles that selfishly consumes the planet's resources. We should all live in a way that considers others and not at their expense. So what should the church's attitude be and what can we say to an increasingly anxious world. Is there anything else the Bible says to guide us? Yes there is!

In Paul's letter to Romans in a passage looking to future he wrote '... *the whole creation has been groaning as in the pains of childbirth right up to the present time' (8 v 22)*. Even in Paul's time before cars, plastics and so on he says the planet (creation) was groaning. We could say that the planet 'groaning' is an appropriate description of what we see today. But this groaning is not because of climate change, it is labour pains for something to be birthed and that is a new heaven and earth. Here is the surprising truth that creation has always been groaning not just in our age. We need to understand why and what will change things. In the same chapter he says *'The creation waits in eager expectation for the sons of God to be revealed' (v 19)* and *'the creation itself will be liberated from its bondage to decay and brought into the glorious freedom of the children of God' (v21)*. The planet's deliverance from decay will be when the full number of God's children is finally revealed at the end of time. This should make it clear that rather than getting caught up in all the forms of save the planet, however well meant, we should be concentrating on preaching the gospel so that people get saved and are numbered with the children of God for our final revelation. Then our present planet will truly be delivered from decay to be replaced by the new heaven and earth.

Jesus in talking about the end times said *'And this gospel of the kingdom will be preached in the whole world as a testimony to all nations, and then the end will come' (Matthew 24 v 14)*. To put it another way: Our priority is to save people not the planet!

CHAPTER 6:

REJECTION, ACCEPTANCE
AND APPROVAL

W hen Jesus was baptised in the River Jordan two remarkable things happened. As He came up out of the water the Holy Spirit descended upon Him like a dove and a voice from heaven said *'This is my Son, whom I love; with him I am well pleased' (Matthew 3 v 17)*. This was a very public loving affirmation by God the Father of His Son Jesus. God the Father was showing pleasure in His Son before He had done any miracles reminding us that God's love is not about what we do but who we are! This was an audible voice heard by those who were present but it wouldn't have been for Jesus' benefit (He would have already known His Father loved Him), it was for ours so we would know who Jesus is and could realise God's desire for deep and loving relationship with man. Don't we all want that kind of security in knowing that Almighty God loves us for who we are?

Our deep inner longings for relationships based on love, acceptance and approval were birthed at creation. God made Adam, who at first was on his own, then God said *'It is not good for the man to be alone' (Genesis 2 v 18)* and we know He then created Eve. This built into mankind the inner longing for relationship not isolation. See the lengths people will go to satisfy this longing. There are dating websites for the lonely of all ages and young people connect with others on social media to feel accepted and have a sense of belonging to mention just two examples. Everyone can relate to this need because it is hard wired into us. But when it doesn't happen or goes wrong it can have long lasting effects that can sour our lives. If it goes wrong we can easily feel rejected and that can have an emotionally crippling effect on us. Some children feel unwanted or they don't measure up, even told they were a 'mistake' or the wrong gender (e.g. we wanted a boy but you are a girl). This is painful and can blight the rest of our lives because no one wants to be unwanted or rejected. This is not and never has been God's attitude towards anyone as He made mankind to share life with Him. So where did it go wrong?

What happened in the Garden of Eden is the root of all mankind's problems. When Adam and Eve disobeyed God by eating from the tree of knowledge of good and evil it resulted in them being banished from the Garden. It removed them from the continuous intimate presence of God as their relationship with Him had been broken. A short while later we come across Cain who having murdered his brother Abel was punished by God and consigned to be without a place to call home. Cain then says '... I will be hidden from your presence; I will be a restless wanderer on the earth...' (Genesis 4 v 14). I know we are not all murderers but I think he voiced the human condition: Hidden from God's presence and restless as we seek fulfilment for our lives. But the good news starts here as God never gave up on getting us home to live with Him forever and He would send His own beloved Son into this world to do it.

God's answer to turn things around was to enter into the human condition Himself through His Son Jesus. Then He could fully experience all the trials of human life to break the power of them over us so that they do not have to blight our lives. In the great Messianic prophecy of Isaiah it says, referring to Jesus, 'He was despised and rejected by men' (53 v 3). Jesus was rejected by His own people of Israel including the religious leaders of the nation, who were the very ones waiting for the Messiah. Instead of recognising and accepting Him, He was rejected and turned over to be crucified by the Romans. Jesus didn't experience rejection just so He knows how painful it is but so that He could take it to the cross to destroy its power over those who would believe in Him. In the gospels I see how Jesus took on the mantle of the Son of Man (i.e. our representative) when He entered the Garden of Gethsemane setting aside His rights as Son of God fully stepping into our shoes. Everything He endured from that point was to break the power of every rotten human experience. He was betrayed, abandoned by His friends, unjustly accused, beaten, abused and crucified.

And ultimately to take responsibility and the judgement for the world's sin on the cross. So Christ has taken the worst rejection it is possible to have so we don't have to suffer its results.

But God doesn't only deal with our past He is most concerned with giving us a good future with Him. He wants us to experience His acceptance and loving approval. In Paul's letter to the Ephesians he spells out the wonderful blessings we receive when we believe in Christ as our Saviour. He explains that there are no limits to the blessings we receive when we believe in Jesus and, emphasising God's heart for relationship, that we are *'adopted as his sons through Jesus Christ, in accordance with his pleasure and will' (1 v 5)*. Notice that when we believe in Jesus He knowingly chooses to adopt us as sons. He also says God did this out of His love for us! It is amazing that we find God had already planned all this before we even decided to accept His Son as our Saviour and that it gives Him pleasure to do this. Can there be a better revelation of the loving heart of Father God? We have dealt with rejection and now acceptance as His 'sons'. But what about approval because we know none of us live perfectly?

In that marvellous opening to Ephesians Paul explains that all the blessings and acceptance are *'freely given us in the One he loves' (v 6)*. Here is the key: all the acceptance and approval are wrapped up in Christ and when we receive Christ we get all that He has and is! Know this: When you believe in Jesus as your Saviour, God the Father looks at you 'in Christ' and He doesn't see you apart from Him but in Him. So you are as accepted and approved of as Jesus is, there is no difference. This is perfect acceptance and approval and we are loved just as Jesus is. Paul put it like this: *'For you died, and your life is now hidden with Christ in God' (Colossians 3 v 3)*. God has done everything necessary through Jesus so that we don't have to suffer the pain of rejection anymore by knowing His perfect acceptance and approval in His Son.

CHAPTER 7

FULL OF GRACE

The simplest of words can contain gloriously rich meaning. John's gospel begins with him telling us how Jesus was the Word who became a man and that He was *full of grace and truth' (1 v 14)*. Consider the word 'full', in this context it doesn't just mean a specific quantity and no more. Even one dictionary catches this thought by describing it as meaning 'abundant in supply' and that is certainly true when we are talking about the grace of the Lord Jesus Christ. God's grace is more than just enough, it is an inexhaustible supply to meet our needs. The Amplified Bible brings this out, *'For out of His fullness (abundance) we have all received (all had a share and were all supplied with) one grace after another and spiritual blessing upon spiritual blessing and even favour upon favour and gift (heaped) upon gift' (John 1 v 16)*. God's grace is a river not a reservoir and can never run dry and was opened up to us by Jesus! This makes it plain that God isn't stingy, He is generous to the max. I will put it like this: Grace is the unlimited supply of God's favour and blessing even though we are undeserving of any good thing from Him. In the world there is lack but not in the Kingdom of Heaven. I write all this to dispel any idea that grace means only just enough.

When Jesus came into the world He brought a new revelation of the goodness of God in all He said and did. In the Old Testament people would talk about the mercy of God but the word grace barely gets a mention. The people of Israel knew about the Mercy Seat that was above the Ark of the Covenant but they had yet to understand that God sat on a throne of grace in heaven (see Hebrews 4 v 16). Jesus came to bring to a conclusion the way of relating to God through law -keeping by ushering in the era of God's grace where we relate to Him simply by believing in the One He sent. Jesus demonstrated the abundance of grace in the things He did. At Cana He created about 600 litres of fine wine from water for the already merry wedding guests. When He called Peter to follow Him He gave him a catch of fish so great it started to sink his boat. On two occasions Jesus created food for thousands of people with much left over. All these occasions demonstrate the wonderful generosity of God's grace. As New Testament believers we need to see everything through the lens of God's grace. We do not live in a conditional relationship with God where He answers only according to our good behaviour because Jesus met all the requirements on our behalf. We qualify for God's blessing and favour when we realise we don't deserve anything. That's what grace is.

So what is the purpose of this wonderful grace? Paul wrote to the Corinthian church to give instruction on what to do with God's grace, particularly in the area of giving. He first of all described how unlimited it is: *'And God is able to make all grace abound to you, so that in all things at all times, having all that you need, you will abound in every good work'* (2 Corinthians 9 v 8). This leaves no need unmet by God's grace so we are not meant to be limited in what we are called to do for Him. Paul then goes on to say *'You will be made rich in every way so that you can be generous on every occasion ...'* (9 v 11). So this is what we are to do, be generous as He is generous. We are meant to be 'river people' sharing God's grace with those in need or as some have said 'blessed to be a blessing'.

CHAPTER 8

NO CONDEMNATION

We are very familiar with the words of Jesus in John 3 v 16: *'For God so loved the world that he gave his one and only Son, that whoever believes in him shall not perish but have eternal life'*. But do we also take note of what He goes onto say in the next verse which is *'For God did not send his Son into the world to condemn the world, but to save the world through him'*. Do we get what Jesus is saying here, He has come not to pass judgment on people but to rescue them for heaven? He further explains in His conversation with Nicodemus that although men do evil deeds deserving of judgement His arrival as Saviour changes the grounds of condemnation by God. See this important statement: *'Whoever believes in him is not condemned, but whoever does not believe stands condemned already because he has not believed in the name of God's one and only Son' (v 18)*. That means that the way out of condemnation is to believe in Jesus as our Saviour because He took the judgment for us. The deciding point is whether we believe in Jesus not our tally of sins. This is further emphasised when Jesus was explaining the ministry of the Holy Spirit to His disciples when He says *'... he will convict the world of guilt in regard to sin ...' (John 16 v 8)*. Note that 'sin' is singular not plural which begs the question what particular sin is He referring to? The next verse (v 9) reveals it *'... in regard to sin, because men do not believe in me ...'*. That is the work of the Holy Spirit today. It is not to condemn people because of their sins (and there is a lot of sin around) but to bring them to a saving knowledge of Jesus. This is what should shape our preaching of the gospel to a very sinful world.

It is very easy to highlight what is wrong in the world because there is so much that distresses us about what goes on. And I am not saying sin doesn't matter, it does because it destroys lives. God makes it plain that He hates sin and what it has done to mankind which is why He sent Jesus into the world. This prompts the question about what should the church's response be to all the bad things that go on around us. As we are called to be light in a dark world we do need to stand up for what is right and a good example is William Wilberforce's successful campaign to end the evil of slavery. But it is not to be a substitute for our prime calling of making Jesus known. Just ending evil behaviour doesn't save anybody because only believing Jesus will do that. Standing up for what is right is part of the church's ministry but is limited to life on earth whereas salvation is for eternity. There is something else to say about how we stand against evil and that is we condemn what they do but not the person. Remember, Jesus came to set people free and bring them out of condemnation. That is true for everyone because '… *all have sinned and fall short of the glory of God*' *(Romans 3 v 23)*. We all were in the same pit once and needed saving. Our desire must be to see people receive the forgiveness of all their sins to experience the freedom of God's complete acceptance through faith in Christ.

It is instructive to see what was actually preached in the church at the beginning and we have two particular sermons recorded to help us. Both are by Peter as the church's primary evangelist. His first is at Pentecost to all who had come to Jerusalem for the feast. He is preaching to Jews under the Law of Moses and would have been aware of what had happened to Jesus. He begins by explaining that the commotion caused by the arrival of the Holy Spirit was simply what had been prophesied by Joel (in other words totally scriptural). He then moves on to say that Jesus had been sent by God and that all that had happened to Him was in line with His foreordained plan. He continues by quoting from Psalms to demonstrate that all that Jesus suffered had been foretold exactly. He concludes by emphatically stating that the one they had crucified was their Messiah. In response to the crowd's distress at this revelation Peter announced that they should turn to Jesus to be saved. Wonderfully around three thousand did and were baptised into the church. Notice that Peter didn't harangue them with a long list of sins, even though they had rejected their Messiah, he concentrated on telling them that Jesus was sent by God, it was all prophesied and that accepting Him as Saviour would bring them out of condemnation. That was to the Jews who had conspired to have the

Romans crucify Jesus. What about to non-Jews like most of us, is it any different? We have another sermon of Peter to a centurion named Cornelius and his household and this time he needed a vision from heaven to persuade him to go to a Gentile's house (it was a no-no for a Jew to consort with a Gentile). This time Peter gives a summary of what Jesus did under the anointing of the Holy Spirit, how He was crucified but resurrected on the third day and that God appointed Him judge of the living and the dead. Then he just manages to say that forgiveness of sins is received through believing in Him when the Holy Spirit interrupts by falling on all who heard him. Again they are baptised into the church. And again notice that Peter doesn't talk about any particular sins they may have committed. He simply wants to put Jesus as Saviour of the world in the spotlight.

I think that the simple point of making sure that our gospel preaching centres on the good news of Jesus rather than rounding on sins and people who commit them is the Biblical pattern to follow. I also believe that is when we see the same results that they saw in the early church.

CHAPTER 9

TRADITIONS

We are all familiar with traditions. We have family traditions, national ones and even churches hold to them. For most of us it is the wallpaper of our lives with the reason for some traditions lost in time but still resolutely held to. We describe some churches as traditional implying that they hold to a familiar and established routine. This usually means there won't be too many surprises if you visit them! The very word means 'handing down' which exactly describes how tradition works. You carry on what has been done by previous generations. But just in case we more adventurous ones think that we are unhindered by tradition, we should realise that there are pentecostal, charismatic and all manner of non-conformist ones as well. Traditions can be established surprisingly quickly when we feel we have hit on a comfortable format and choose to continue it week after week, year after year. But the question is do traditions help or hinder? If you don't think this is an issue try suggesting something that changes a fondly held tradition in your church.

Let us look at what happened when Jesus bumped into the traditions of the religious elders in Israel, which is recorded in Mark chapter 7. Having heard what was happening in Galilee some Pharisees and Scribes came down from Jerusalem to check Jesus out, but not with a Berean attitude. When they saw the disciples eating without washing their hands they jumped on this as a violation of the 'traditions of the elders'. To you and me this would be about good hygiene but to them it was a religious compliance issue. They turned a good habit (washing hands) into a tradition (we always do this) and into a religious requirement (you must do this). Washing hands before eating is sensible hygiene (particularly in a pandemic) but they had turned it into a religious ritual. Jesus is uncompromising in His response to their criticism. He quotes from Isaiah exposing their hypocrisy of 'honouring God with their lips while their hearts were far from Him'.

He further points out that these traditions were made by men and not the commands of God. And He doesn't stop there as He exposes how these religious fanatics used their traditions as a cover for their own corrupt behaviour. We know from other confrontations Jesus had with the religious rulers that outward obedience to their traditions were used to look good in front of people, and a way of masking their inner moral bankruptcy. It was a pathway to the self-righteousness that God detests. This is challenging stuff so perhaps we need to see how it could apply to us.

I have no doubt that some traditions have value. Traditionally we meet together on a Sunday to worship together and hear the word preached. We also regularly take communion together to focus on Jesus and remember what He has done for us. Tradition can also put a framework in place in our services so things don't get chaotic (see Paul's letter to the rowdy Corinthian church to see the guidance he gives). All these are helpful but there are ways traditions are used that are definitely not good and downright dangerous. When keeping traditions are more important than responding to God, and are also seen as the way of keeping right with God rather than faith in Christ this is a problem. Traditions can also be used as a subtle way of excluding people who don't fit our profile of acceptable ways (read how the religious viewed 'sinners' in the gospels). A sobering case to study is the thief on the cross next to Jesus. At his recognition of who Jesus was and his own need of salvation, he was promised that he would be with Him in paradise that very day. The thief had no opportunity to get baptised, take communion, read his bible, put on his best clothes to go to church or anything else yet he received the great reward for his faith in Jesus. He had no chance to keep any traditions! Traditions in themselves are not the problem it is what we do with them that counts. Are they a shield to hide behind or are they a help to keep us focussed on Jesus? I write all these things not because I am against good tradition as I like order (ask my wife!), but so that we don't let them get in the way of our relationship with God or we don't let them become a substitute for intimacy with Him.

CHAPTER 10:

MANKIND'S IDENTITY CRISIS

It is the most natural thing in the world to search for identity. Children dream about what they want to do when grown up and who they want to be like. And there are no shortage of options on offer in today's media saturated culture. They are presented with a blizzard of alternatives about who they want to be even down to sexual identity! Another hallmark of our age is an obsession with celebrity. People enthusiastically pursue it, presumably hoping it will be their ticket to a prosperous and fulfilling life together with the adulation of their admirers. We are dazzled by internet sensations and TV programmes capitalise on this appetite for fame. But the tragedy is people actually lose sight of their true God given identity in the clamour for significance. But this not only applies to those who lust after fame as everyone has a longing for identity. So what has gone wrong?

As with all the world's problems it went wrong in the Garden of Eden. Mankind lost its sense of true identity when Adam and Eve disobeyed God's command not to eat from one particular tree in the middle of the garden. In the beginning when God created man He said *'Let us make man in our image, in our likeness ...' (Genesis 1 v 26)*. This was man's original identity so they could truly represent Him in their stewardship of the world. But this image was corrupted when, deceived by the serpent, they disobeyed God. They were tempted with the lie that if they were to eat the forbidden fruit *'will be like God' (3 v 5)*. Think about what they were being told. The serpent (Satan's mouthpiece) was saying if you disobey God you will be like God! That is crazy logic, but sadly the deception worked and we all live in the fallout of that disobedience today. That day mankind lost its original God given identity and has been searching for it ever since. What has the Bible got to say about all this?

The answer the Bible gives is opposite to the way the world thinks. When Jesus was talking to His disciples He said *'If anyone would come after me, he must deny himself and take up his cross and follow me. For whoever wants to save his life will lose it, but whoever loses his life for me will find it. What good will it be for a man if he gains the whole world, yet forfeits his soul? Or what can man give in exchange for his soul? (Matthew 16 v 24 – 26).* It is important to note the significance of the word 'soul' here. The soul is understood to mean our mind, will and emotions which is what establishes our individual identities. Jesus is saying if you want to find your true identity let go of pursuing a worldly counterfeit that cannot truly satisfy. He says you can have the whole world at your feet yet have nothing of any real value. Jesus says embrace His will and purpose for our lives then we will find our true selves. And these aren't only principles that Jesus is passing on, He lived this out. Jesus is God the Son yet He humbled Himself and became the Servant King (see Letter to Philippians chapter 2). One man who discovered his true identity is the apostle Paul. He makes a profound statement to the Galatian church: *'I have been crucified with Christ and I no longer live, but Christ lives in me. The life I live in the body, I live by faith in the Son of God, who loved me and gave himself for me' (2 v 20).* There is so much in this verse but what is clear is that Paul let go of the ambitions of his old life and embraced God's will for him. As a result he found his real identity as someone loved by God called to be the greatest church builder in history. But that wasn't just meant for Paul as his experience is there to teach us that as we also embrace God's will and follow Jesus we will find our true identity and purpose here on planet earth.

When this happens there is a surprising and powerful result. John chapter 17 records Jesus' final prayer before His arrest. He prays for Himself, His disciples and everyone who later would believe in Him, and that includes us. He prayed *'I in them and you in me. May they be brought to complete unity to let the world know that you sent me and have loved them even as you have loved me' (v 23).* We can see that when there is unity with God and with other believers it is an announcement to the world that Jesus is the Christ and Saviour of the world. Like Paul when we completely identify ourselves with Jesus and allow the Holy Spirit to live the 'Jesus' life through us it brings us into the quality of unity with Him that He prayed for. This is what finding our true identify in Christ is for. Finding our true identities establishes unity in the church and is evangelism! This truth is also found in Psalm 133 where it says where there is unity it is like the flow of anointing oil (a picture of the Holy Spirit) and results in God releasing salvation. We can now see why our enemy works so hard to promote division as a truly united church breaks his evil grip on people. Finding our true God given identity might not seem to be of great importance but I believe, as I have argued above, it has the potential not only to change our own lives but our nation too.

CHAPTER 11:

WHO CAN YOU TRUST?

Trust is a very valuable thing. It is the confidence that what a person or organisation says is true and what they promise to do they really will do. When that happens we say they are trustworthy. Companies make a lot of efforts to convince you to trust the claims they make for their products and services. Political parties go into overdrive to convince you that they are the ones you can trust in government and that they (not the other lot) are the trustworthy ones! Clearly gaining trust and being seen as trustworthy is still prized today. We can see that it all starts with what we say. It begins with words and they have real power to generate trust when we follow through and deliver on promises made. This is very relevant for the church in its mission to preach the gospel.

But there is a problem. All the efforts the world makes to persuade people of trustworthiness reveal that there is a problem of lack of trust. Our default position has become one of scepticism and a need to be convinced with solid evidence before we will trust anything or anyone. See the explosion of conspiracy theories on the internet to see the scale of mistrust. If this was just about material things we buy or services we pay for we would say it is just being wise with our money. So not a big issue. But it doesn't only effect material things, as a lack of trust can have a devastating impact on reputations and relationships. One lie, when exposed, can destroy trust that has been built up over years, and modern media spares no-one when these things are revealed.

This prevailing sceptical atmosphere presents a challenge for the church in preaching the gospel to today's world. In our increasingly secular societies many people don't even believe there is a God let alone believe in what He says. Scandals, reinterpretation of the Bible, emergence of religious cults have led many to distrust what the church says. There is nothing new here as it all began when Satan (via a serpent) said to Eve in the Garden of Eden *'Did God really say ...' (Genesis 3 v 1).* That is where distrust was born. Today it translates into 'can you really trust what the Bible says'. Satan's aim is to discredit God with the lie that He is not truthful with us so cannot be trusted. This is why preaching the gospel is not only a matter of truth but of trust in the integrity of God and His word. God says what He means and means what He says and He has given us what He says in the Bible. In Hebrews chapter 6 it says when God was making promises to Abraham *'since there was no-one greater for him to swear by, he swore by himself' (v 13).* God swore an oath to give a guarantee that He would keep His promise, and He has! It goes on to say that there are two reasons why God always keeps His word. He makes an oath and *'it is impossible for God to lie' (v 18).* Do we get that? It is **impossible** for God to lie, men may lie but God cannot because it would contradict who He is. This is both an assurance and a challenge.

A few years ago I was wondering what it would take to see a major move of the Holy Spirit in this nation. As soon as I had voiced that question I had an immediate response: 'When My people take Me at my word'. A simple answer with profound implications. When the disciples took Jesus at His word and preached the gospel they saw salvations, miracles, healings and the church exploded into life. And so it has been throughout the centuries as the promise still stands. Yes, God is the One we can trust as He is trustworthy and His words remain forever! Will we trust in His word?

CHAPTER 12:

IMITATING OR LIVING THE LIFE

In chapter 8 of Paul's letter to the Roman church he reveals God's predestined plan for believers. He writes that it was His purpose that we *'be conformed to the likeness of his Son' (v29)*. This means God planned for us to do what Jesus did, preach the good news, cast out demons, heal the sick and so on. But being made like Jesus means much more than just the outward actions. See how the Amplified Bible translates that phrase: *'moulded into the image of His Son (and share inwardly His likeness)'*. This means our likeness to Jesus is to be more than just skin deep, we are to be like Him on the inside. God's plan is for a complete transformation of our lives so that our attitudes and motives together with our actions are just like Jesus. Paul called it being *'sons of God' (see 8 v 14)*. In other words we are not to just imitate Jesus but to live the Jesus life. Let us be clear, this is impossible for us out of our own abilities or determination as we need the Holy Spirit to do something radical in our lives to make it happen. Fortunately we have the life and writings of Paul to help us understand how we can reach that place of oneness with Christ. Which is something He prayed for (see John 17 v 23). We will also need the Holy Spirit to give us personal revelation as we explore Paul's experience because we are talking about something supernatural that is obscure to the natural mind.

There are important insights woven throughout his letters. In Colossians he reveals that the 'mystery' of the gospel is *'Christ in you, the hope of glory' (2 v 27)*. When we accept Jesus as our Saviour He comes to live in us by the Holy Spirit which also guarantees that we will be with Him in glorious eternity. Knowing that Christ lives in us is the key and foundation for living the Jesus life. In Galatians Paul makes a profound statement: *'I have been crucified with Christ and I no longer live, but Christ lives in me. The life I live in the body, I live by faith in the Son of God, who loved me and gave himself for me' (2 v 20).* We can see three truths in this amazing statement:

1. Paul saw that his old life died with Christ on the cross.
2. Paul had a brand new life with Christ living in him.
3. This new life is a life of faith in all that Jesus had done on the cross and His resurrection.

Any idea that Paul's new life is merely a cleaned up and improved version of his old life is out of the question. The heart of the gospel is death to the old life so we can be born again to a Christ filled life. He expands on this in Philippians when he bluntly states that he considered his privileged Hebrew heritage and past achievements as rubbish compared to gaining Christ (3 v 8). He continues saying that his desire is to fully share life with Christ so that he becomes like Him (3 v 10). His passion and love for Jesus is so great that he wants to share in His sufferings, recognising that Christ laid His life down for others. Knowing how Paul lived and the opposition he faced we could easily think we could not live like that. And neither could he if it wasn't for the grace God gave him to do it. God will always give us the grace we need to live the lives He calls us to. We should also take encouragement that Paul was humble enough to say he hadn't perfected all this but was pressing on to take hold of all that Christ had for him (3 v 12 – 14).

Our reactions to the challenge of living such a Christ centred life reveal a major obstacle we all have. The problem is that our natural thinking struggles to accept the spiritual reality of all that Christ has done for us. Spiritual realities are not understood by the natural mind they are revealed to us by the Holy Spirit and not by human reasoning (see 1 Corinthians 2 v 9 – 10). But Paul comes to our aid once again in Romans: *'Do not conform any longer to the pattern of this world, but be transformed by the renewing of your mind. Then you will be able to test and approve what God's will is – his good, pleasing and perfect will' (12 v 2).* Paul exhorts us to ditch worldly wisdom and attitudes and line up our thinking with what God says. Then our thinking will change to line up with Him and His plans for us will become clear. The gateway to all this happening is found in the preceding verse which urges us to offer up our whole lives to God as an act of worship. It is what Paul did as a worldly wise Pharisee and we know the results it produced.

That brings us to what will be the results of a life lived like this? The simple answer is fruit! When Jesus was giving His last teachings to the disciples He said '... *I chose you and appointed you to go and bear fruit – fruit that will last' (John 15 v 16)*. Jesus wants His disciples (you and me) to bear healthy enduring fruit. I see two types of fruit in this. The first is personal fruit. In Paul's letter to the Galatians he contrasts fruit of the sinful nature (i.e. old life) with fruit of the Spirit which is *'love, joy, peace, patience, kindness, goodness, faithfulness, gentleness and self-control' (5 v 22-23)*. These are all expressions of the Jesus life because they are characteristics of Jesus Himself. But it is a relief to see that they are fruit of the Spirit which means we don't have to produce them we simply carry them. As Jesus put it, we are branches connected to Him that carry His fruit (see John 15). A life lived like this will have an impact which brings me to the second type of fruit. I started this letter referring to the statement in Romans 8 v 29 that said God's plan was for believers to be made like Jesus. The verse goes on to say *'that he might be the firstborn among many brothers'*. God's intention was that Jesus would open the door for many others to follow Him into heaven and the way it would happen would be through multiplication. The early church grew through the Spirit filled lives of believers with their testimony of the gospel. And God has not changed His method so it can happen today when we follow in their footsteps and live Jesus filled lives.

As I close, let us remember that our loving Father is not asking us to live an impossibly challenging life but inviting us to share one of intimacy with Him together with the satisfying fruit of multiplication. What an invite!

CHAPTER 13

THE GATEWAY GIFT

As Christians we are familiar with the word righteousness. But do we fully comprehend what it means for us and its importance. An equivalent word for it is 'just' and some versions of the Bible use it as an alternative translation. When we say a person is righteous or just it paints a picture of someone we judge to be honourable and morally upright in the way they conduct themselves. But how does God call it? When you read the Bible it doesn't take long before you realise that His standard of righteousness is different to ours and demands perfect behaviour in all things. In our thoughts, words and attitudes as well as actions. But is all this simply a theological detail? After all our culture today seems to be satisfied as long as people are mostly moral (politicians rely on this attitude!). But what should we think about this and what does the Bible teach us?

Righteousness is a foundation of God's kingdom. In Psalm 89 we find this revelation: *'Righteousness and justice are the foundation of your throne ... (v 14).* God's throne is built on perfect righteousness and if there was any unrighteousness at all it would collapse and the universe with it. That is how important it is, not just to God but also to our security. And you cannot separate righteousness from God as it is part of His nature. Being counted as righteous is also the requirement for us to be able to stand in the presence of God without sin separating us. Again from Psalms: *'Open for me the gates of righteousness; I will enter and give thanks to the LORD. This is the gate of the LORD through which the righteous may enter' (118 v 19-20).* This means that to be where God is we must go through a gate that only the righteous may enter. These Old Testament verses are prophetic as no-one was able to freely enter God's presence under the Law of Moses. The construction of the tabernacle, sacrificial system and ritual restrictions were a cover to protect Israel from His judgement of their unrighteousness. God shielded Himself from Israel as a safeguard so He could still be with them. What this all means for us is, that we must be counted as righteous by God to be accepted without fear of judgement. But the cross has changed all that for us as we no longer have to produce our own righteousness to gain entrance to His presence.

In Isaiah's great Messianic prophecy it says *'by knowledge of him my righteous servant will justify many, and he will bear their iniquities' (53 v 11)*. This points to Jesus who took responsibility for all our sins at the cross and, most significantly, justify us before God. So not only did Jesus take our punishment for sins but also made us righteous, just as if we have never sinned. This reveals the crucial truth that righteousness is a gift and not earned. The apostle Paul put it like this in his letter to the Roman church: *'For if, by the trespass of one man, death reigned through that one man, how much more will those who receive God's abundant provision of grace and of the gift of righteousness reign in life through the one man, Jesus Christ' (5 v 17)*. Adam's sin may have released the curse of death into the world but through Jesus Christ we receive the gift of righteousness and eternal life though the grace of God. It is so like God to use Paul to reveal these truths as he was extreme in trying to produce his own righteousness. In his Philippian letter he itemises his Hebrew credentials and efforts to pursue a legalistic righteousness, but explains it was to no avail and worse than useless. After he had met Jesus he could write that he did not have *'a righteousness of my own that comes from the law, but that which is through faith in Christ – the righteousness that come from God and is by faith' (3 v 9)*. So here is the answer to how we are righteous: We are righteous when we believe in Jesus as our Saviour.

We are counted as righteous in God's eyes by faith in Jesus Christ alone not by any effort of our own. See this extraordinary statement Paul makes to the Corinthians in his second letter: *'God made him who had no sin to be sin for us, so that in him we might become the righteousness of God' (5 v 21)*. God the Father put all the world's sins on His own Son as the final once and for all sacrifice so that we would be spared His judgment and, as a result of believing in Jesus, we are called the 'righteousness of God'. What a precious gift this is. Also as you continue to believe in Him you are still counted as righteous irrespective of what you do as it by faith not by deeds. This is simply because Jesus is our righteousness and He doesn't change and the cross stands forever. When you know you are righteous (your position before God not your performance) you know your God given rights as a child of God. These are tangible rights not just abstract doctrine. Consider what Paul says in the letter to the Romans, having explained in detail what God has done through Jesus he writes *'Therefore, since we have been justified through faith, we have peace with God through our Lord Jesus Christ'* (5 v 1). Knowing we have peace with God has a powerful effect on us mentally, emotionally and physically. Even secular doctors agree that any turmoil in a person's life has a significant impact on their health. When we have peace with our creator we can survive life's storms. But we want more than just survival we want to thrive, so look at this promise from Psalms: *'For surely, O LORD, you bless the righteous; you surround them with your favour as with a shield'* (5 v 12). This is a promise to protect and prosper us simply because we are righteous in God's eyes. When we believe this promise and take a stand on it, even though circumstances or opposition may try to contradict it, this remains a right of the righteous.

I have argued that righteousness is so much more than a theological truth, it is a gateway to God's best for you. Picking up on the quotation from Psalm 118 again, God **has** opened up for us *'the gates of righteousness'* (118 v 19). He did it through Jesus at the cross and is offered to all as a gift.

CHAPTER 14

BEYOND FORGIVENESS

We live in an unforgiving world. I know that is a bleak statement but personal experience and what we see around us sadly confirms it. I am sure many, if not all of us, will have experienced unforgiveness at some level. Either others have not forgiven us or we have not forgiven someone. With the world's hat on we would say some things are unforgivable and they should remain so. Furthermore, the thinking is that to forgive would excuse the offence and that would be unjust to the offended. Even the world recognises that trying to bridge the gap between offender and offended is essential if we want to see peace and not conflict. But this will always be limited to reconciliation rather than genuine forgiveness as something more profound has to happen in the human heart first. Sadly, unforgiveness is a tragic reality of our world but forgiveness is a very powerful truth that can literally transform lives. What is God's perspective on this?

First we need to consider our own need for forgiveness before we tackle the challenge of forgiving others. The Bible is emphatic '... *all have sinned and fall short of the glory of God' (Romans 3 v 23)*. Every human being who ever lived needs God's forgiveness irrespective of how big we think our sins are. The world fools us into thinking that as long as we are mostly good and don't do anything seriously evil we are OK with God. But that is not His standard. To be acceptable to God you must be perfect in all ways (thought, word, attitude and deed). Our problem in understanding this is because we only look at the sins committed and not the root cause. We sin because we have a sinful nature that we all inherited from Adam. See what Paul said to the Roman church: *'Therefore, just as sin entered the world through one man, and death through sin, and in this way death came to all men, because all sinned... (5 v 12)*. There is no escaping our human heritage. We are born with a nature that is independent from God and bent on doing our own thing however smartly dressed up. So our first need is to be forgiven by God and that is the heart of the gospel.

Our forgiveness was announced at the last supper when Jesus took the cup of wine and said *'This is my blood of the new covenant, which is poured out for many for the forgiveness of sins' (Matthew 26 v 28).* His blood paid for our sins and provided forgiveness by God. When we see Jesus on the cross and the cost of forgiveness do we realise how much we have all been forgiven? It was the human race that put Him on the cross not just a few bad individuals. But when we believe in Jesus as our Saviour we receive that forgiveness and it changes everything. And knowing we are forgiven positions us to forgive others. But God doesn't only require us to forgive others, He goes further than forgiveness. See the words of Jesus from the Sermon on the Mount: *'But I tell you who hear me: Love your enemies, do good to those who hate you, bless those who curse you, pray for those who ill treat you' (Luke 6 v 27-28).* This is exactly what Jesus did when He forgave those who crucified Him and then died for them. But how is this possible for us? Has anyone ever managed to do this?

In the book of Acts we read how Stephen, as he was being stoned by the religious leaders, prayed for God to not hold this sin against them (Acts 7 v 60). That is forgiveness in action. Also there are moving testimonies of people who have chosen to forgive when terrible things happened to them or their families. They have realised that to live in unforgiveness would have consumed their own lives in bitterness and kept them anchored in the painful memories of the past. For them it was not about forgetting but choosing to forgive. In some cases, where it was possible, they visited the perpetrator to show that forgiveness and relieve them of crushing guilt. There are even cases where they have been accepted into the families they harmed. How did they do this? All of them would say they needed God to supply the grace to make it happen. And here is the answer, God will supply all that is necessary to forgive and bless those who have hurt us but He won't do it without our permission. God never takes away our free will but when we surrender it to Him in any area of our lives He provides whatever we need. This sounds simple but it is the truth.

When we say to God I don't feel like forgiving someone but I decide to do it we find there is a release of His grace that enables us to not only forgive but makes it possible to pray for and bless them. But there is more, because as we choose to forgive others we discover that we experience a wonderful release. We are set free from the past holding us back, free from toxic emotions and free to move forward into the future.

Moving beyond forgiveness is liberating for ourselves, as well as others, and starts with a decision. Then God's grace can flow and do what we thought was impossible. All because of what Jesus did on the cross.

CHAPTER 15:

THE COMPETITION FOR ATTENTION

This is a very simple point: What we give the most attention to shapes our lives. A good example is an Olympic athlete who will dedicate a good few years of their life to the dream of winning a medal. We know that their whole daily routine revolves around attaining and maintaining peak fitness for their chosen discipline and it will involve everything that has an influence on their performance. This means diet, exercise routines, sleep patterns and most of all time. The dream will have their complete attention because it is that important to them. To many of us that seems extreme, but we all prioritise what we want to focus on. We decide what is important to us and try to gear our lives around that desire whether it is family, job, sport or whatever else. But we live in an age of unprecedented competition for our attention whether it is what to buy, where to go on holiday, what to watch and even what you should think. Today's media is designed to draw you in to what it wants you to see and hear. Have you noticed how in some TV ad breaks the sound level goes up as they try to draw you in to their message or product! The risk of all this is that our attention is spread so thinly that we don't have the ability to engage with anything in depth. We are not talking about whether we can multitask here but our ability to focus. What we may not realise is that this competition for attention will steal time and energy from what is really important. We need help to balance our lives so we can give the right amount of focus to what really matters. Let us see what Jesus teaches us about what is going on here and what we can do about it.

Jesus said He had come to give us 'fullness of life' but that Satan comes to steal (see John 10 v 10). This reveals that we have an enemy, and one of his tactics is to steal our time and energy so that we cannot experience the abundant life Jesus promised. The story of Mary and Martha illustrates this point. Mary sat at Jesus feet to listen to Him while Martha became distracted by all the preparations necessary to host Him. After complaining that she was left to do this on her own, Jesus told her that Mary had made the right choice in giving her undivided attention to Him (see Luke 10 v 38 – 42). It is not that Martha was wrong, but that she was missing a blessing by doing the right thing at the wrong time. Jesus also told an important parable likening the word of God to seeds. He explained that *When anyone hears the message about the kingdom and does not understand it, the evil one comes and snatches away what was sown in his heart. (Matthew 13 v 19).* We now see that Satan wants steal the gospel message so people cannot be saved. Jesus goes on to say, that others who hear the message of the kingdom but are overcome by 'troubles' give up and those distracted by the 'worries of this life' and 'deceitful of wealth' don't experience fullness of life. Our enemy uses the tactic of distraction to steer us away from the truth and the life Jesus brings us. The incessant competition for our attention is his sneaky way of doing this. This brings us to the question of how to shape our lives so we can live with kingdom focus when there all the other demands on our time.

At this point it is vital to make clear I am **not** suggesting a 'you must do this' list of actions, because it is all about our relationship with Jesus and not a method. All Christians know about the importance of prayer, reading the Bible and meeting together to worship. Also there is a wealth of Bible teaching on the TV and internet which we can choose to use to build a kingdom foundation in our lives. What I am suggesting is about increasing the depth of our intimacy with Jesus. His desire is that we should know Him as He knows us. In His prayer before arrest Jesus said *Now this is eternal life: that they may know you, the only true God, and Jesus Christ, whom you have sent' (John 17 v 3).* This means that the gift of eternal life is to know Him and the Father. This sounds like we have to totally dedicate ourselves to seeking Him to the exclusion of all else, and that only church leaders have the opportunity to do this as we have so many other things to take care of. It will help us to remember that the apostle Paul made tents as he travelled around preaching and teaching, and he definitely had a deep relationship with Jesus. So there must be ways to have an intimacy with Him that is compatible with our responsibilities in life. This is not impossible as, when we believe in Jesus, the Holy Spirit comes and lives in us permanently. So He, God the Holy Spirit is with us and in us all the time, 24/7. I call it having a 'continuous conversation' with Him throughout the day whatever I am doing. I can ask Him to give me revelation when I read the Bible. I can ask Him to show me how to pray about a situation. I can talk to Him or pray in tongues in the car. I even ask Him to show me the best way to do DIY when I am flummoxed. I can even shut up and just listen for what He might want to say! It is just the same as being with your family, naturally talking with them throughout the day. Now here is the surprising thing, as we cultivate this awareness of the Holy Spirit we will find that our kingdom focus will sharpen. We will be less distracted by the competition for our attention and still be able to fulfil the responsibilities of our daily lives. I am convinced this a recipe for the 'fullness of life' that Jesus wants us to have and we may be surprised at what good things may happen.

CHAPTER 16:

SALVATION CONTROVERSIES

S alvation is the great gift of God. When we accept this gift we are saved from judgment of all our sinfulness and given a new eternal life with Him. All this was paid for by the once and for all sacrifice on the cross of God's own Son Jesus Christ. This is the gospel, that God was removing the barrier of sin to bring us back to Himself. But as with all the great truths in the Bible there are controversies over how we interpret what salvation really means for us. In this letter I look at four different understandings about how we are saved that have existed in the church over the ages. Controversy has occurred because there are verses that can be used (or misused) to support these different interpretations. So let us be Berean and look at the different ideas on salvation.

Controversy 1:

'Jesus died for everyone so all are saved whatever we do'. This is usually referred to as Universal Salvation. This sounds attractive as it would mean we all go to heaven no matter what we do. The danger with this is that it breeds complacency because we don't need to do anything to be saved. But that ignores what Jesus said about Himself: *'For God so loved the world that he gave his one and only Son, that whoever believes in him shall not perish but have eternal life' (John 3 v 16)*. Believing here means to completely put your trust in someone not just know about them. Jesus also points out that not believing in Him means we perish, that is we don't go to heaven. In other words no automatic salvation. John put it like this: *'Yet to all who received him, to those who believed in his name, he gave the right to become children of God' (John 1 v 12)*. It is clear that we have to believe and receive Jesus to be saved. It is apparent that Universal Salvation is a wrong understanding of salvation.

Controversy 2:

'We are saved by being good and doing good deeds'. This is rooted in the Old Testament with the covenant of law that applied to Israel. Under the Law of Moses you had to obey God's rules to be right with Him. This principle was then applied to salvation meaning you had to obey God and do the right thing to be saved. As long as you did the outward obedience you were OK. This view, that salvation is in our hands, was deeply entrenched in the church until the Reformation and sadly still lingers today. The big problem here is that it produces uncertainty because you don't know if you have done enough to be saved. And there are other issues, as some who think they have done well will become proud and some who think they haven't will feel guilty. Furthermore, when we feel guilty we end up in an endless cycle of asking for forgiveness without the assurance that we have been forgiven. Regrettably, it also opened the door for pressure to be put on people to 'perform' to make their salvation sure. The mistake here is that it ignores the new covenant of grace made by the death and resurrection of Jesus. The Old has been replaced by the new as stated in Hebrews: *'By calling this covenant "new", he has made the first one obsolete; and what is obsolete and ageing will soon disappear' (8 v 13)*. We can't relate to God under a defunct covenant. Paul explains the new covenant as follows: *'For it is by grace you have been saved, through faith – and this is not from yourselves, it is the gift of God – not by works, so that no-one can boast' (Ephesians 2 v 8-9)*. Salvation is based on accepting what Christ has done for us and not on what we do. The Reformation began with the rediscovery of 'righteousness by faith alone' and this truth still needs to be preached today to expose the fallacy of salvation by works.

Controversy 3:

'God predestines who is saved and who is condemned'. Also called Unconditional Election. This thinking is usually associated with Calvinism and Reformed Theology and is based on a particular interpretation of the word 'predestination'. It emphasises God's Sovereignty (His right to do whatever He wishes without reference to anyone else) but downplays the

New Covenant announced by Jesus at the last supper. This doctrine applies predestination to man's eternal destiny and infers that Christ only died for the ones that God had already decided were to be saved, the so called 'elect'. How valid is this idea which still has a strong following today? The word predestination is only found in two books of the New Testament (Romans & Ephesians) and in both cases they are addressed to believers and not as a warning to the world. The key statement here is found in Romans where Paul writes *'For those God foreknew he also predestined to be conformed to the likeness of His Son' (8 v 29).* Here we see that predestination is not about our destiny but about the transformation of our lives into the likeness of Jesus. This controversy confuses God's foreknowledge with His will. Just because God, with His perfect foreknowledge knows who will accept Jesus as their Saviour doesn't mean it is His will that people perish. He wouldn't give us free will if it didn't make any difference to our destiny. Peter made it clear in his letter that God is *'not wanting anyone to perish, but everyone to come to repentance' (2 Peter 3 v 9).* When we believe in Jesus we are then elected into His family to be predestined to be changed to be like Jesus. The danger with Unconditional Election is that it will inevitably lead us to form judgments about who we think are earmarked for salvation and be indifferent to those we judge don't make the cut. God is not into selection but election into His family.

Controversy 4:

'We are saved by grace but we have to work out our salvation to keep it'. This is a very prevalent view in the church today because it seems only right that Christians must live godly lives. It is obvious that as believers we should conduct ourselves in ways that honour God but does the security of our salvation depend on us living obedient lives? Most Christians would accept they don't live perfect lives but as long as they keep on confessing their sin they will still be OK (see Berean Letter No.2 for more on this). The root issue here is, once you believe in Jesus can you somehow lose your salvation by doing something bad or not doing something good? If we think this is possible it will produce insecurity because we are never sure we have done enough to stay saved. This all arises when we confuse the Old Covenant with the New Covenant to create a mixture of law keeping and grace. This is not a new problem as Paul had to write a very strong letter to the Galatians because that is what they were doing. We are all familiar with the phrase 'falling from grace' which is usually applied to someone who commits a big sin. But see how Paul defines it: *'You who are trying to be justified by law have been alienated from Christ; you have fallen away from grace' (Galatians 5 v 4)*. So 'falling from grace' is when you rely on law keeping for justification. Not only is it useless, it separates you from Christ. Trying to justify yourself to God by keeping any rules, rituals, traditions or doing good deeds rejects the work of the cross whether you are saved or not. What did Jesus say about the security of our salvation? In John's gospel He said *'My sheep listen to my voice; I know them, and they follow me. I give them eternal life, and they shall never perish; no-one can snatch them out of my hand. My Father, who has given them to me, is greater than all; no-one can snatch them out of my Father's hand. I and the Father are one' (John 10 v 27-30)*. What a promise of security, we are locked in the hands of Jesus and the Father. Where should we put our trust, in our ability to keep ourselves saved or in God's promise to keep us? I think the answer is obvious. The truth is we are saved by grace through faith to live by grace through faith.

I am convinced that God wants us to be secure in the knowledge of the grace that is ours in the Lord Jesus Christ. *'May the grace of the Lord Jesus Christ, and the love of God, and the fellowship of the Holy Spirit be with you all' (2 Corinthians 13 v 14)*.

CHAPTER 17:

WHY CONTEXT IS IMPORTANT

How do we view the Bible? Is it a timeless book detailing God's dealings with mankind and the people of Israel in particular? Is it full of stories that can be used to teach us about how we should live life? Or does it have a bigger message about living on earth and a life beyond? The Bible itself makes a very clear statement about its origin and purpose: *'All Scripture is God breathed and useful for teaching, rebuking, correcting and training in righteousness, so that the man of God may be thoroughly equipped for every good work' (2 Timothy 3 v 16-17).* By its own definition, God inspired men to write down His words in the various books of the Bible for us to read. And not only is it helpful for Christians, we know it also has a message for the world. The issue we are looking at here is how we accurately interpret the Bible's message. If God has made sure we have His written word we need to understand what He is saying and what it means for us.

When we read the Bible we need to know the context to properly understand its relevance for us. Context is all important because when things are taken out of context they can not only lose their true meaning but end up seeming to say the opposite of what was intended. In any passage we need to know; who was it talking about, what the situation was, where it took place and when it all happened. To illustrate this we can remember that in the Old Testament the Law of Moses was specifically given to the people of Israel and not to Gentiles. This means any Mosaic laws or requirements don't apply to non-Jews as they were not intended for them. In the gospels, Jesus, when He sent out the disciples said don't go to the Gentiles but go to the *'lost sheep of Israel'*. But then in Acts He says go into all the world and has to instruct Peter via a vision to preach the gospel to Cornelius (the first Gentile convert). Seeing the context makes sense out of seemingly contradictory facts. There is another dimension here for Gentiles to grasp. Virtually all the Old Testament and the majority of the New is framed around a Jewish heritage and culture. If we aren't familiar with all the nuances of this we can miss a lot of rich meanings in the text. It is a real blessing when a Jewish believer explains the cultural background to what is in the Bible.

A theme often used by preachers, which can so easily be taken out of context, is when Jesus talked about 'the sheep and the goats' (Matthew 25 v 31 – 46). I have heard this misused and have got cross because of the way it can coerce people into good works and cause anxiety about their eternal destiny. Because it follows two other parables (the 'Ten Virgins' and the 'Talents') it can be presented as though it is a parable meant to teach all us how we should live and do good to others (see verses 35 – 36). But is not a parable, as Jesus was making a prophetic statement about something that was going to take place in the future. Note how He starts by saying *'When the Son of Man comes in his glory, and all the angels with him, he will sit on his throne in heavenly glory' (v 31)*. Jesus is referring to a specific event in history that is yet to be seen. This is when He will return to deliver His people Israel from their seven years of tribulation. It goes on to say *'All the nations will be gathered before him ...' (v 32)* which is when He separates people on earth as 'sheep' and 'goats' to pass judgement on them. This judgment relates to how nations treated His people Israel in those traumatic seven years. This is confirmed by His statement: *'whatever you did for one of the least of these brothers of mine, you did for me' (v40)*. By using the term *'these brothers of mine'* He is emphasising that He is a Jew, born into the tribe of Judah and He is talking about the treatment of His countrymen. The reason why ignoring this context is dangerous is because of the fate of those categorised as 'goats'. They *'will go away to eternal punishment'*. It is just plain wrong if this passage is used to motivate people to do good things as not only is it manipulative, it can make a believer fear hell itself if they don't perform! Knowing the true background here makes all the difference.

This why it is vital to know the context of what we read in the Bible so we have a correct understanding of what God is really saying to us.

CHAPTER 18:

WHERE ARE YOU LIVING?

In the Bible we can see different phases of world history unfolded for us. The first chapters of Genesis chronicle creation and the emergence of various people groups that become the nations of the world. The focus then moves to one particular group, the nation of Israel. The majority of the Old Testament is about God's dealings and the covenants He makes with them. But there is also an important sub text woven into the story and that is the changing role of mercy, grace and law.

Let us look at some instances that demonstrate what I am talking about. In Genesis chapter 4 we see Cain murdering his brother Abel. God shows mercy by not demanding his life as a punishment and then grace by promising protection against revenge (see 4 v 15). Under the covenant God made later with Noah, Cain would have been executed. Mercy and grace were the prevalent basis of justice until the Law of Moses was established. From then on we see God dealing with Israel on the basis of obedience to laws with penalties for disobedience. At the same time we see God showing mercy to Ninevah when they repented from their evil behaviour (see Jonah 3 v 10). When we move to the New Testament we see the revelation of God's purpose in history in bringing us into the time of grace. At the expense of His own Son, Jesus Christ, God's undeserved favour and blessing is released to us. What I see is how God, at the beginning, reveals His heart by showing mercy and grace to mankind. Tragically, because of mankind's sinful nature it doesn't respond to Him but rather becomes worse (see Genesis 6 v 5-6). He now moves to pick out one particular people (Israel) to demonstrate two things. The first is to see what life is like with God protecting, providing and blessing even though they don't deserve it. And the second, by giving the Law of Moses, is to show it is impossible for man to live perfectly because his nature is corrupt from birth. All of this is to show we need God's grace because nothing else will do to put us right.

It is interesting to see that this shift from mercy to grace to law and back to grace is mirrored in church history. When the church was birthed it was moving in mercy and grace with wonderful things happening. Then when the Christian faith became the state religion of the Roman Empire it sank into legalism until the Reformation. The rediscovery of salvation by faith alone brought it back to the cross and the gospel of grace. But that wasn't the final stage as at the beginning of the twentieth century we had the birth of Pentecostalism followed by the Charismatic movement. This reminds us that grace is an ever flowing river and will never settle until history is concluded. This changing pattern of church doctrine is also reflected in the different denominations we see today. The reason I think all this is relevant is because people like to identify themselves with groups or denominations and that produces mind-sets that determine attitudes and behaviour. Here is the problem, if I live with an Old Testament mind-set I will emphasise the keeping of the Ten Commandments and have a legalistic attitude. If I picture myself in the gospels I will try to follow the teaching of Jesus but struggle to experience the peace of knowing I am right with God. If I see myself in the fifty days after the cross before Pentecost I now have peace with God but yet to see the power to live the new life. Finally I move beyond Pentecost and discover the power of the Holy Spirit to live this born again life to the full. I also discover that this is the purpose of God's grace for me. So where are you living?

CHAPTER 19:

THE MOST DANGEROUS WORDS EVER SPOKEN

I f we want to know how important words are we should see this statement from Proverbs: *The tongue has the power of life and death ...' (18 v 21)*. Words can build up or tear down, bless or curse, enlighten or deceive. Genesis tells us that God created the heavens and the earth by speaking words but we also see that our enemy also knows the power of words. His name Satan means accuser, revealing that he also operates by words. Look at this conversation in the Garden of Eden between the serpent (Satan's agent) and Eve: 'He said to the woman, *"Did God really say, 'You must not eat from any tree in the garden'?"' (Genesis 3 v 1)*. Those four words *'Did God really say'* are the most dangerous words ever spoken! They opened the door to doubt and unbelief in who God is and what He has said that has continued to this day. Even when people do believe in God they can doubt that God's promises are true or for them. Doubt is a subtle but very effective weapon that our enemy uses against us to edge us into full blown unbelief. The world and media broadcast false ideas and untruths that continually contradict what the Bible says. Our modern culture is swamped with things that encourage doubt in simple Bible truths, for example do we believe in creation or the theory of evolution? It even gets presented in theological garments, when we are encouraged to not take the Bible literally but more as allegories. The point is, we are immersed in an environment that fosters doubts designed to rob us of what Jesus died to give us.

But there is nothing new here. When Jesus went to the Bethsaida a blind man was brought to Him for healing. He took the man by the hand and led him outside the village and restored his sight. He then told him not to go back into the village but go home. Now the question here is, why did Jesus take him outside the village and why did He tell him not to go back? I believe it is because in the village he would have been surrounded by doubt and unbelief which would have made it harder for him to receive his sight (it took two goes anyway!). If he had gone back he may have faced scepticism about his miracle that made him doubt and lose his healing. Again, when Jesus raised Jairus's daughter why did He send the crowd away and only take her parents, Peter, John and James into the room with Him. It was to eliminate any atmosphere of doubt that could have hindered the miracle. Another instance, which reveals an important truth, is when Jesus delivers a boy from an evil spirit. The boy's father asks if Jesus can help and He replies *'Everything is possible for him who believes' (Mark 9 v 23)*. The father's response is illuminating: *'I do believe; help me overcome my unbelief' (9 v 24)*. The father's honest answer demonstrates something that is true for all us; he had faith and doubts all at the same time! We could put it like this: He knew Jesus could heal but would He do it for him? What this tells us is, that if we believe in Jesus as our Saviour we already have saving faith but can struggle to see that faith work in the everyday. It is doubts that can grow into unbelief that is the problem. The issue is how to get rid of our doubts?

The answer is very simple. What do we fill our minds with? See Paul's well known advice: *'Do not conform any longer to the pattern of this world, but be transformed by the renewing of your mind. Then you will be able to test and approve what God's will is – his good, pleasing and perfect will' (Romans 12 v 2)*. When we switch off the world's input and turn on God's input our doubts will start to disappear and we can confidently say to our 'serpents', YES, GOD DID SAY!

CHAPTER 20:

WHAT IS LIFE FOR?

The gift of life is something God gives and I have yet to meet anyone who says they arranged their own birth. Before anyone points it out, there is one exception and His name is Jesus whose birth was planned before the beginning of time. But thinking about our lives, if we see life as a gift it prompts the thought of what do we do with it? If you believe in a God who created us, an obvious question would be why am I here, what is my life for? As believers we know that when we accept Jesus as our Saviour we receive the gift of eternal life (John 3 v 16). Which means that when we leave this earth we shall go to be in heaven with Him for eternity. But as we still have our days here on earth before that happens we want to understand what we should be doing. Most of us want to know the specifics of what God wants us to do so we can get busy, but I think the way it comes about is not so obvious. That is what I want to try and explain in this letter because it is counter intuitive and we can get the 'cart before the horse'.

One person may say our life is to serve and they picture themselves as servants of God. They argue that Jesus our Saviour made Himself the Servant King so we should follow His example. But notice what Jesus said to His disciples: *'I no longer call you servants, because a servant does not know his master's business. Instead, I have called you friends, for everything that I learned from my Father I have made known to you'* (John 15 v 15). Here is an important insight, the disciples served from a place of intimacy with Jesus. Without that intimacy there is a remoteness, as though waiting for the next assignment to be sent down. Serving without intimacy is hard work and not what God intends. His desire is that we serve out of oneness with Him with His power and by His grace. Serving will be the fruit of our relationship with Him and not the basis.

Another may say our life is to glorify God. Is glorifying God a work? If it is, let us play wall-to-wall worship music and paint 'Glory to God' on everything! Now don't get me wrong, worship has its rightful place in our lives and it is good to openly give praise to Him. I'm talking about how we glorify God in our everyday lives. Look at an instruction Paul gave to the Corinthian church: *'So whether you eat or drink or whatever you do, do it all for the glory of God' (1 Corinthians 10 v 31)*. Here is the answer to how we glorify God in everything we do, whatever and whenever it is. Glorifying God is an attitude we can all have not a work to do. In simple terms, it means always giving Him the credit for what we do, whether it is our job, sport etc. As before, the greater our intimacy is with Him, the more you will see His power at work in our lives and the more you will realise He gets the glory.

This brings me to the conclusion of what our life is for. Jesus provides the answer in His prayer recorded in John 17: *'Now this is eternal life: that they may know you, the only true God, and Jesus Christ, whom you have sent' (v 3)*. He gives us the reason we are gifted eternal life. It is to know the Father and the Son in the deepest possible way. Our lives here are so we can begin to know God intimately. When this comes first everything else falls into place, whether it is serving or glorifying Him. Sadly, this is the opposite to how many of us approach this issue. Let us make intimacy with Jesus our priority then we will see wonderful things happen that will glorify Him.

CHAPTER 21:

APOSTASY OR REVIVAL?

There is an end time paradox that divides theological opinion on how events will work out before the rapture of the church. Over several decades there have been prophecies, visions and expectations of a mighty end time revival. A 'great awakening' that will usher millions into the Kingdom of God. There is the Smith Wigglesworth prophecy of 1947, the Tommy Hicks vision of the 'Awakening Giant' in 1961 together with more recent prophecies given through others (details of all these can be found on the internet). But to counter this expectation some point to what Paul wrote to the Thessalonians when they became disturbed by false reports that they had missed the rapture (increasing persecution made them think they had entered the Great Tribulation). He corrected their misunderstanding by saying: *'Let no one deceive you by any means; for that day will not come unless the falling away comes first, and the man of sin is revealed, the son of perdition' (2 Thessalonians 2 v 3 NKJV)*. The NIV expresses *'falling away'* as *'the rebellion'*. Paul explains that there will be an apostasy before the rapture of the church and the appearance of the antichrist. Two thousand years later and all this is yet to happen. So here is the question, can they both be true? Can there be an apostasy and a great revival?

Let us first consider the apostasy Paul talks about. If people have fallen away we are speaking about people considered to be part of the church not people of the world. We know that there are those who are connected with the church but are not necessarily born again believers. They are often referred to as nominal believers i.e. those who subscribe to the moral and ethical values of Christianity without a personal commitment to Christ. I describe this as Christian by preference rather than conviction. Is this who Jesus talks about in the parable of the sower? He mentions those who don't understand, those who fall away due to trouble or persecution and those overwhelmed by the worries of life or worldly gain.

Sadly the Bible makes it clear that there will be some who fall away even when they have heard the gospel and that before the rapture there will be a recognisable apostasy. Whether this will be due to a specific event or a gradual thing has yet to be revealed. A valid question would be whether those who fall away were really saved in the first place. But rather than blame people for falling away perhaps we should take an honest look at what we the church have been preaching and teaching. Have we been true to the gospel of grace? After all, we see in the Book of Acts how many were soundly saved by the preaching of the gospel in the power of the Holy Spirit, even when the disciples were being heavily persecuted and there was pressure not to become a Christian. Throughout history revivals have brought salvation to millions and even changed nations. As I see it, God has not shut the door on all this yet so revival in the face of apostasy is possible. We are also reminded that God is *'not wanting anyone to perish, but everyone to come to repentance' (2 Peter 3 v 9)*. God's heart is to save people not condemn and that is why He sent us Jesus. Wouldn't He do everything possible to give everyone a chance to respond? The question now is, can I find Biblical evidence to support the idea of a great end time revival even with apostasy.

Lets start with Peter's Pentecostal sermon. He quotes the over 800 year old prophecy of Joel in which God promised to pour out His Spirit. That first Pentecost announced the beginning of the 'last days' which we are still in until the rapture and return of Jesus. But there is something important to see in this familiar passage and that is, who does the promise refer to? See the beginning of the quotation: *'In the last days, God says, I will pour out my Spirit on all people. Your sons and daughters will prophesy, your young men will see visions, your old men will dream dreams.' (Acts 2 17)*. Notice the phrase *'all people'* which the Amplified version translates as *'all mankind'*. This infers an unrestricted pouring out of the Holy Spirit onto all not just the church and notice the prominence given to young people (*'sons and daughters'* and *'young men'*). I can imagine gatherings with unbelieving young people, who under the sound of the gospel experience the Holy Spirit falling on them. And that they are so radically changed they begin to prophesy and have visions. Isn't this what was promised? See this closing verse in Mark's gospel: *'Then the disciples went out and preached everywhere, and the Lord worked with them and confirmed his word by the signs that accompanied it' (Mark 16 v 20)*. If this is so we must see our young people as the great opportunity for revival and not a problem group. We must also accept that they will do things differently to us! Another reason why I think this is true is because of how the Joel prophecy continues: *'Even on my servants, both men and women, I will pour out my Spirit in those days, and they will prophesy' (Acts v 18)*. The way this is written draws a distinction between the *'all people'* of verse 17 and *'my servants'* of verse 18. This can only be referring to us as believers, who have been given the responsibility of preaching the gospel of grace. Also we should notice how Peter's quotation of Joel's prophecy ends: *'And everyone who calls on the name of the Lord will be saved' (Acts 2 v 21)*. Surely our emphasis must be to faithfully preach the gospel to all mankind expecting to see an end time revival even though there will be an apostasy.

None of us know exactly where we are on God's end time clock but we are warned to note the signs of the end described in the Bible. There is definitely a growing expectation that the rapture is on the horizon as we see end time Biblical events unfolding in the world. What should our response be to this? I believe that all this can be an urgent catalyst for an awakening of the church. We need a fresh revelation of the glory of our Lord Jesus just like John had on Patmos. We need reminding of the completeness of the victory Jesus won for us on the cross and the position of authority He has put the church in to represent Him in the world. And we need to experience the unlimited power of the Holy Spirit working in us and through us as we make Jesus known. When this happens Jesus will be centre stage in the church in all things and all other priorities will be relegated to be of secondary importance. We will realise this is happening when we see praise and worship of Jesus raised to a new, never seen before level. This will be a mighty revival and apostasy will not stop it. One final thought, doesn't history tell us that God only needs a handful of people to turn the world upside down? So are we ready and willing?

I now rest my case. There can be both apostasy (as clearly mentioned in the Bible) **and** a mighty revival before the church is taken away to be with Jesus. But I want my focus to be on the revival so that people have every opportunity to receive salvation!

CHAPTER 22:

WAVELENGTHS

The gospel truths never change. They are established forever and are the incorruptible foundations of our faith. As Paul wrote *'For what I received I passed on to you as of first importance: that Christ died for our sins according to the Scriptures, that he was buried, that he was raised on the third day according to the Scriptures'* (1 Corinthians 15 v 3-4). He is reminding the church that he received a revelation direct from the Lord Jesus of the grounds of our salvation. He says this is of *'first importance'* meaning we need to hold this uppermost in our understanding. When speaking to the disciples after His resurrection, Jesus gave us the content of the gospel message *'He told them, "This is what is written: The Christ will suffer and rise from the dead on the third day, and repentance and forgiveness of sins will be preached in his name to all nations, beginning at Jerusalem ..." (Luke 24 v 46-47)*. Our gospel message is to be: Repent (change the way you think), believe in Jesus as you Lord and Saviour and you will receive the forgiveness that He won for you at the cross. This seems clear enough, but there is something to see in how we engage with people of different mind-sets. In the gospels we see how Jesus spoke in different ways to different people. One example would be the woman caught in adultery by the religious Jews (see John 8 v 1-11). Jesus didn't condemn the woman even though she had clearly broken the Law of Moses whereas He challenged the religious over their self-righteous attitude. To the one He spoke the language of grace to the others the language of law. And there are other examples too. Contrast how He spoke to the rich ruler (Luke 18 v 18-25) with Zacchaeus (Luke 19 v 1-10). Again we see how He spoke to one in the language of law to the other the language of grace. Now we know Jesus came to save all people and is not prejudiced towards any one. What we see is how He knows how to tune into where people are at. I picture this as speaking to people on a wavelength they can hear, just like dialling into a particular radio station. I think this is vital to reaching different groups who seem to be impervious to the gospel we preach.

My view is that the modern western culture, typified by the millennials (those born from the year 2000 on) is on a different wavelength to previous generations. Our young people have grown up in the internet age with an unprecedented input of different world views which has created attitudes and ways of thinking that have dramatically moved away from our norms. The gospel centres on Jesus as *The Lamb of God who takes away the sins of the world'* but how relevant does that seem to millennials where understanding of right and wrong has become blurred. But how did we get to the place where the difference in wavelengths between the generations has become so big? As always, we find the root of the problem in the Garden of Eden. The serpent tempted Adam and Eve to disobey God with the lie that *'you will be like God, knowing good and evil'*. Not only was our independent nature birthed that day but crucially the beginning of mankind's desire to decide what is good and what is evil independent from what God says. Over the ages several things have come in like serpents to change people's thinking. I think that the evolution vs creation is a particularly destructive attack on the very idea of a creator God. The theory of evolution is taught in science lessons but creation is relegated to religious studies, at best. We can see the way evolution thinking leads: Evolution means no creator, no creator means no God, and no God means we decide what is right and wrong! That is why to some abortion is not wrong it is a free choice issue on how they want to live. Paul expresses what is going on with what he wrote to the Corinthian church *'The god of this age has blinded the minds of unbelievers, so that they cannot see the light of the gospel of the glory of Christ, who is the image of God.' (2 Corinthians 4 v 4)*. Satan has deceived young people with multiple God denying ideas dressed up in all manner of human rights issues and justifiable causes. These, together with the desire to decide right and wrong for themselves has desensitised them to what God calls sin. They don't recognise Paul's incredibly accurate description of a downward moral spiral we see when society rejects the existence of God (see Romans 1 v 18-32). What we see as disturbing they see as progressive. Here is the question: How do we talk to this generation on a wavelength that they will tune into?

On TBN Christian TV station they run a trailer which shows interviews with young people and their views about God. While this is obviously only a sample, they all reject the idea of God and instead say they rely on themselves or friends in the challenges of life. But paradoxically several are open to the idea of meeting Jesus, which shows how confused they really are! They also express fears of being alone in this world which I believe indicates as to where they are really at. It seems to me that the most important thing for them are relationships. Just look at what this internet savvy generation is hooked on: Social media, TV reality shows, TV soaps etc. They all major on relationships and how they do or don't work out. Here is the irony, the gospel is all about restoring a broken relationship with God. The very thing they are deaf to will give them the best and most wonderful relationship with God. Right at the creation of man God said *'It is not good for man to be alone. I will make a helper suitable for him.' (Genesis 2 v 18)* and *'.. a man will leave his father and mother and be united to his wife, and they will become one flesh' (Genesis 2 v 24)*. We were created for relationship! The Trinity is a relationship, Father, Son and Holy Spirit and we are made in His image. So even in a God denying generation they still are expressing something that He seeded in us all. If relationship is the name of the game for the young generation we need come in on that wavelength.

Could it be that to reach the millennial generation we need to come in on the line of restoring relationship with God rather than the forgiveness of sin? After all, forgiveness of sin is simply the means of restoring relationship but the purpose is peace with God. Perhaps if we emphasise the majesty of Jesus and the wonder of who He is in our preaching it will draw young people to Him. If they fall in love with Him and accept Him in their lives then all the other questions about forgiveness of sin, creation, attitudes etc. will be resolved as they open up their lives to Him.

CHAPTER 23

DIVERSITY

We talk about diversity in nature, that wonderful variety in God's creation of animals, plants, scenery etc. But this seemingly innocuous word has become a pressure word in modern culture and its purpose is to change the status quo. An illustration of this is the pressure put on the film industry in the controversy over ethnic representation, particularly with the Oscars. This is not an argument for keeping things the same as some things do need to change where there is injustice and prejudice. But the diversity banner is also being used to push for agendas that are blatantly at odds with God's purposes for mankind. Diversity is being used as a pressure to accept a wider range of gender identities and sexual orientations that contradict God's creative order of male or female. Is this just a sign of the times or is something more serious at work here?

What is God's perspective on diversity? After all, as already said, there is a beautiful variety in creation which means there is such a thing as good diversity. Let us go back to His original intent at creation. When God created man it says we were made in His *'image'* and *'likeness' (Genesis 1 v 26)* so that we could share a harmonious life with Him. However this plan was frustrated by the corruption of human nature at the fall which destroyed this harmony with God. But He already had a redemption plan to recover the situation, although it would need His sovereign intervention to ensure it would be fulfilled. This is seen at the flood, when God saw that the wickedness of man had become so great (see Genesis 6 v 5) and because of the interference of fallen angels (*'sons of God' Genesis 6 v 2*) He needed to rescue Noah and his family. Noah was counted as righteous and blameless in his generation so would provide the new human line for a Saviour to come through. Then we come to the God's intervention at the Tower of Babel. Now man had become so arrogantly ambitious that they wanted a tower to reach the heavens and make a name for themselves (see Genesis 11 v 4). In other words *'to be like God'* which was the serpent's deceiving temptation in the Garden of Eden (see Genesis 3 v 5). So God thwarted man's ambition by confusing their language and scattering them all over the earth. This created the diverse languages and cultures we see today! Now He starts to unfold His rescue plan. Out of this diversity He makes a covenant with one particular person Abraham, to not only be a father of nations but also to be the line (the nation of Israel) from whom the Saviour will come. This is fulfilled through the Lord Jesus and His death on a cross. Now a door out of corrupt diversity has been opened that can bring us back to harmony with God. So what about a godly diversity?

When we accept Jesus as our Lord and Saviour we enter into a lifelong journey of being *'conformed to the likeness'* of God's Son (see Romans 8 v 29). This prompts the question, what is the place of diversity in God's Kingdom? At this point we need to realise that being made like Jesus is not the elimination of personality, as we can see that no people called by God were turned into clones. Also, Jesus prayed that those who believed in Him would be united and one with Him (see John 17 v 20 – 23). This was evidenced in the early church which was described as being *'one in heart and mind' (Acts 4 v 23)* even though they were a diverse group of people. Unity is not uniformity. I believe this shows this is all about having a harmony of attitudes and motives. Perhaps the best way of explaining what this looks like in real life is to see it as the fruit of the Holy Spirit listed in Galatians: *'love, joy, peace, patience, kindness, goodness, faithfulness, gentleness and self-control' (5 v 22 -23).* That is exactly what Jesus is like and who we are being made like. This is possible for all believers whatever their background or personality. I think this all adds up to meaning that good diversity is simply the variety of godly personalities.

But a godly diversity is not Satan's agenda at all. He wants to corrupt what God wants and counterfeit what He does. He caused the corruption of man's nature through the temptation to sin which made us follow his and not God's ways (see Ephesians 2 v 1 – 2). The counterfeit was to try and form us into his image and likeness. If we want to see what this looks like in real life we only have to see what the *'acts of the sinful nature'* are (see Galatians 5 v 19 – 21) which is a depressingly accurate description of what we see around us today. Satan is using the apparently reasonable tolerance of diversity to cause confusion in society today. This matters because it has the potential to divide the church as it will soon be backed into a corner to say whether it will accept the sexual and gender diversity demands. Some will say we need to accept diversity to be relevant in today's world while others will say we must stick to what God says is right. But the real purpose of this attack is to divert the church from preaching the gospel by entangling it in interminable wrangling over sexual morality. This is why the diversity issue is important.

The truth is that the church should let what God says be the last word on all this. But there will be a cost in this stand as we could soon be accused and even charged with 'hate speak'. We might not be physically persecuted in the western world but, make no mistake, this is a subtle attack on our Christian faith. Whatever happens, may the Good News of Jesus still go out in power!

CHAPTER 24:

THE APOSTASY

The Bible says that in the end times before Christians leave to be with Jesus and the appearance of the Antichrist, there will be an apostasy (see 2 Thessalonians 2 v 3). This is variously translated as *'the rebellion'* (NIV) or *'the falling away'* (NKJV). The Amplified version adds this explanation *'… the predicted great falling away of those who have professed to be Christians …'*. Clearly something very significant will happen as some will abandon what they say they believe in. I do not think that this means that those who are truly born again will lose their salvation but refers to those who merely 'profess' to be Christian (i.e. they subscribe to the moral and ethical values of Christianity but have not made Jesus Christ their Lord and Saviour). I also don't believe that the apostasy precludes an end time revival (see Berean Letter 21 for more on this). But we need to see what apostasy looks like and more importantly how it will happen so we can avoid being sucked into it. Jesus warned us that that in the end times we need to be watchful so that we are not deceived and also to understand how to interpret the signs of the times (see Matthew 24). This letter is an attempt to discern what the Bible tells us about this important end time issue.

The apostle Paul wrote to Timothy about what would happen in what he called the last days (see 2 Timothy 3 v 1-5). He gives a disturbingly comprehensive description of Godless behaviour which sadly is often the theme of what is now considered entertainment. I used to think that Paul was only talking about what goes on in the world around us but this is not correct. In verse 5 of this passage he says this applies to those *'having a form of godliness but denying its power'* meaning this is talking about those who have connected themselves to the church. This sounds like a description of apostasy to me. Again, I think this refers to those who outwardly align themselves with Christianity but inwardly have not been renewed. They do not have the power of the Holy Spirit to live the born again life. For me, it says there is a great need to preach the truly life changing gospel in the church as much as to the world! But how is this all going to come about?

In a previous letter (number 21) I commented that whether the apostasy was triggered by a specific event or was a gradual thing was not clear. I have come to the conclusion that it is because of both issues. For an individual a specific event could be responsible. It might be a personal crisis where they are disappointed that God didn't seem to come through for them or a worldwide disaster (like the Covid pandemic) that they blame God for. At the same time the osmosis of the world's values into the church sets it up to be open to deception, doubt and unbelief in what God says. The more like the world the church becomes the less we will see of God's presence and power. Paul is really strong in his letter to Timothy about this when he says *'Have nothing to do with them'* (v5). That is a real challenge for us and some would argue it flies in the face of the call to unity. I interpret this as meaning to be on our guard against the inroads of the world into the church and to challenge it when we see it creeping into people's attitudes. Sadly, as he writes elsewhere, if someone isn't receptive to correction we need to disassociate ourselves from them. We shouldn't condemn them but we can pray for them to change as we hope others would do for us if we get off track. The issue is the honour of God's name as we represent Him in the world. What happened to Ananias and Sapphira is a sobering reminder that God is holy and does not want His name dishonoured (see Acts 5). But back to what is the real trigger to apostasy.

This is revealed when Paul begins his description of what apostasy looks like with the words *'People will be lovers of themselves ...'* (v2) and then ends it with *'rather than lovers of God'* (v4). This is the root of apostasy, it is a love problem. The core issue is who do you love more, yourself or God. If it is yourself you are vulnerable to apostasy, if it is God it is a safeguard against it. I am persuaded that increasing evidence of a love of self in the church over a love of God is the sign of the apostasy. Worryingly, this is the hallmark of the self-obsessed times we live in. Is there any other Biblical evidence for this conclusion, and what should our response be?

Paul wrote his letter to Timothy who was pastor of the church in Ephesus. Jesus also wrote a letter to the church in Ephesus which we find in Revelation. He commends them for their hard work, perseverance, testing of false apostles and their stand against wrong teaching (the Nicolaitans). But He also says *'Yet I hold this against you: You have forsaken your first love' (2 v 4)*. So here it is again, a love problem which prompts Jesus to say that if they don't change He will *'remove your lampstand from its place' (2 v 5)*. This is serious, their waning love for Jesus has put them in jeopardy of no longer being counted as a church by Him (*'lampstand'* means church). It is also reasonable to infer that as their love for Jesus has gone so has their love for others. As Paul also points in his famous love chapter (1 Corinthians 13) you can be very busy doing good things, having a major ministry impact but without love it is meaningless. Love is the main thing because *'God is love' (1 John 4 v 16)*. It is the very essence and nature of God. It is what He is all about and why He sent His Son Jesus into the world to save us. The Holy Spirit puts this divine love in us so He can love others through us which reminds that we are not talking about the human level of love (limited and often conditional).

Lastly, are there clues as to when this might all happen? In the last days before His arrest, Jesus gave the disciples an overview of the end times. He describes earth shaking events and severe persecution of the church. All things we see happening today, which convinces many that time is short. Because of this He says *'At that time many will turn away from the faith and will betray and hate each other...' (Matthew 24 v 10)*. That sounds like the apostasy. But notice what He also says *'Because of the increase of wickedness, the love of most will grow cold...' (24 v 12)*. Again love is the crucial factor in how things will go for us. So that we don't despair at the inevitably of all this Jesus also says *'but he who stands firm to the end will be saved' (v 13)*. How we need the encouragement of each other, the grace of God and the Holy Spirit to do this. So what to do and how do we respond?

When Paul wrote to Timothy, having recognised the dangers of apostasy, he gave him a solemn charge: *'Preach the Word; be prepared in season* and out of season; correct, rebuke and encourage – with great patience and careful instruction' (2 Timothy 4 v 2). Paul says whatever is going on, preach the gospel of Jesus Christ. Jesus also puts this emphasis on the priority of preaching the gospel when in His end time overview He says: 'And this gospel of the kingdom will be preached in the whole world as a testimony to all nations, and then the end will come' (Matthew 24 v 14). The conclusion is plain, we are to keep preaching the gospel of the grace of God that is revealed to us through the Lord Jesus Christ. In the light of all that I have argued, I believe we need to emphasise that the gospel is the revelation of His great love for us. If people fall in love with Jesus (who He is not just what He can do for you) then that can be an antidote for the apostasy. May God's love be increasingly revealed through the preaching of the gospel.

CHAPTER 25:

DOES TODAY'S CHURCH AGREE WITH THE APOSTLE PAUL'S TEACHING?

The early church was built up on the foundation of Paul's teaching. As he wrote to the Corinthian church: *'By the grace God has given me, I laid a foundation as an expert builder, and someone else is building on it.'(1 Corinthians 3 v 10)*. This is a bold statement of the authority of his teaching but he later validates this by saying that he had revelation directly from the Lord Jesus Himself. In the same letter, when giving instructions on communion he said *'For I received from the Lord what I also passed on to you …'* *(1 Corinthians 11 v 23)*. Although Paul was not one of the original twelve disciples Jesus broke into his life and personally commissioned him to preach the gospel. It is clear from his writings that Paul was given insight and understanding to enable him to fully explain what Jesus had done for us on the cross. Paul's letters have always been counted as Scripture which means they are part of God's word to us. Even Peter comments on this pointing out that it was because of *'the wisdom that God gave him' (2 Peter 3 v 15)* and that Paul's letters are to be considered as *'the other Scriptures' (v 16)*. What this all adds up to is that his letters are part of our God given yardstick for judging doctrine. But can we say that we, the church, have stayed faithful to Paul's teaching or have we become selective in what we believe? Let us look at three issues to see whether we have deviated from Paul's gospel.

The first issue is: Has God finished with Israel? In 70AD the Romans destroyed Jerusalem along with the temple which led to the people of Israel being dispersed across the world. As all this was a fulfilment of prophetic words by Jesus (Matthew 24 v 1-2) it reinforced a view that God had washed His hands of His chosen people Israel. The logic was, as Israel had rejected their Messiah God had rejected them and for nearly 2000 years it certainly looked like that. They had no country of their own and endured relentless persecution by the world. Sadly, much of the church also embraced anti-Semitic attitudes and doctrines that persist to this day. This is most blatantly revealed in Replacement Theology which is based on the false idea that the church has replaced Israel in God's plans. This is despite the inconvenient fact that our Saviour is Jewish and that the early church was almost exclusively made up of Jews. The foundations of the church are Jewish! But does this replacement idea stand up to scrutiny? An honest evaluation of history has to acknowledge that the rebirth of the State of Israel in 1948 is a remarkable event. How could a nation come into being over night without divine involvement? There was, because this is a fulfilment of prophecy: *'Who has ever heard of such things? Who has ever seen such things? Can a country be born in a day or a nation be brought forth in a moment? Yet no sooner is Zion in labour than she gives birth to her children'* (Isaiah 66 v 8). 1948 was the fulfilment of that prophecy given nearly 3,000 years earlier. But more specifically, what does the apostle Paul have to say on this? In his letter to the Roman church he reveals his distress over the fate of his fellow Israelites who have rejected Jesus as their Messiah (see Romans 9 v 1 – 5). In chapters 9, 10, 11 he details the revelation he was given that showed God had not finished with Israel and that they would be restored in the end times. He explains that Israel had suffered a *'hardening in part' (11 v 25)* for the sake of the Gentiles (also see 11 v 11). We are the beneficiaries of their centuries of alienation and we owe them a debt of gratitude that it was for our benefit. Paul goes on to describe Gentiles as wild branches grafted into a cultivated olive tree (Israel) but warns us not to boast that branches were broken off so we could be grafted in (see 11 v 17 – 24). These natural branches (Jews) can be grafted back in (v 24). In these chapters Paul makes it clear that God has not finished with Israel and the church has not replaced it. In his letter to the Ephesians (2 v 11 – 22) he explains that God's plan is to bring the church and Israel together to be one in Christ as he wrote: *'And in Him you too are being built together to become a dwelling in which God lives by His Spirit' (2 v 22).* It is clear that the idea that God has rejected the Jewish people forever and that the church has replaced them is a serious error and is not supported by Paul's teaching.

We know that righteousness (right standing with God) is a gift we receive when we believe in Jesus as our Lord and Saviour. This raises the second issue: What do I have to do to stay righteous in God's sight? Do I have to make sure I fully obey the Ten Commandments or keep some other rules and rituals? Will I be righteous on a good day but lose it when I mess up? This question had bounced around the church from the very beginning. Paul had to write a stern letter to the Galatian church who had fallen into the error of believing they had to fulfil all the requirements of the Law of Moses as well as believing in Christ. Paul made this startling statement: *'You who are trying to be justified by law have been alienated from Christ; you have fallen away from grace' (Galatians 5 v 6)*. By adding keeping the law to faith in Christ they had turned their backs on Him. It is either law or Christ there can be no mixture. Keeping the law (or any rules or rituals) never produced righteousness, see what Paul wrote to the Roman church: *'But now a righteousness from God, apart from law, has been made known, to which the Law and the Prophets testify. (Romans 3 v 21)*. This error arose because of a misconception of the purpose of the Law, it was not to make us righteous but to reveal our sinfulness and need of a Saviour. Back to Galatians: *'So the law was put in charge to lead us to Christ that we might be justified by faith' (3 v 24)*. So what about keeping the Ten Commandments as a way of living right? We should realise that they are part of the Law of Moses, given at the same time as all the other commands given by God. Paul described them as a *'ministry of death, which was engraved in letters on stone' (2 Corinthians 3 v 7)*. In other words keeping the Ten Commandments or any other rules will only condemn by showing us how incapable we are of right living by our own efforts. It is plain to see that having been saved by faith it is a nonsense to go back to keeping laws, rules or rituals to maintain our righteousness. Paul teaches that our righteousness doesn't come and go depending on our performance as Christians. Our position is set by faith in Christ alone, it is a gift and it is not earned. As we believe in Christ we are counted as righteous, no matter what. Any teaching that pushes us to obey rules or rituals to stay righteous (i.e. saved) is in conflict with Paul's teaching. This leads into the next issue on how to live righteously without falling into legalism.

This third issue is all about the way godly living is produced in us. As stated above, our position of righteousness is set by faith alone but our performance varies as we are unable to live perfectly by our efforts. In other words Christians still sin but we are still forgiven! See Paul's indignant reply to the suggestion that this is a licence to sin (Romans 6 v 1 – 4). Too often we are exhorted to do right and shun wrong and it is easy to pick out Paul's instructions on right living in his letters. But what is often overlooked is that Paul's guidance comes at the end of his letters after he had laid the foundation of the grace that is ours through the cross of Christ. Do's and don'ts never produce the right long lasting results for godly living. This is because legalism actually provokes sin! See what Paul wrote: *the power of sin is the law* (1 Corinthians 15 v 56). This is not widely understood because it is counter intuitive, after all the world needs laws to prevent chaos. But the Kingdom of God does not work like the world does. Now lets see what Paul says about how to produce righteous living. He wrote to Titus in Crete, which was rife with ungodliness, and encouraged him to teach them about the grace that is ours in Christ (Titus 2 v 11 – 14). This is the answer, as we emphasise the grace it changes us so that we desire and are empowered to live increasingly godly lives. Any doctrine that pushes rules contradicts his teaching and will not produce the right results.

CHAPTER 26:

THE BACK STORY

The media often coin new words and phrases to describe things in a way that will attract your attention. One that I have noticed recently is the use of the words 'the back story' which is what we used to call the background. This is presumably based on the thought that people want more than information, they want stories. Stories sell, as an inspection of newspapers, television and the internet will reveal. You could call it an obsession with wanting to know everything about what is going on. When someone becomes famous the media get to work to give you the back story to let you know the how's and why's. If someone is infamous they will dig into the background to suggest what happened in their lives to cause such notoriety. But back stories aren't limited to individuals they are also used for world events. Everyone has a back story, so how should we as Christians view our own journeys in life? Does the Bible have anything to say about having a healthy perspective on all this?

The Apostle Paul's experience is a good place to look as he gives us valuable insights into the way he views his past life. In his letter to the Philippians he gives his back story: *'circumcised on the eighth day, of the people of Israel, of the tribe of Benjamin, a Hebrew of Hebrews; in regard to the law, a Pharisee; as for zeal, persecuting the church; as for legalistic righteousness, faultless' (3 v 4-6)*. Paul described his past life as a religious Jew before he met and believed in Jesus as his Saviour. This intense religious upbringing undoubtedly fitted him well to explain the Old Testament in the light of the gospel. But he goes on to make a dramatic statement about his past achievements: *'I consider them rubbish' (3 v 8)*. We need to bear in mind that the context here is his rejection of his past opposition to Christ and his warnings about those who wanted to impose religious laws on believers. He saw that having got things so wrong before, his desire now was to know Christ and share in His sufferings. But Paul doesn't dwell on his past and said: *'But one thing I do: Forgetting what is behind and straining towards what is ahead, I press on towards the goal to win the prize for which God has called me heavenwards in Christ Jesus' (3 v 13-14)*. It seems that Paul was even reluctant to talk about all he went through for the sake of Jesus. In his letters to the Corinthian church he was provoked to talk about his sufferings when his credentials were being questioned by false apostles (see 2 Corinthians 11). Paul would rather look forward than backward. This poses an interesting question about the way we give our testimonies as Christians. Perhaps the lesson here is that our emphasis must be more on what God is doing in our lives now rather than where we have been, however spectacular our story might be. Also it may not be healthy to keep going over our past lives and reminding ourselves of past hurts and failures. It can even resuscitate unforgiveness towards those who have harmed us. After all Paul also wrote: *'If anyone is in Christ, he is a new creation; the old has gone, the new has come!' (2 Corinthians 5 v 17)*. Maybe the simplest way to put this is that Jesus has taken away our past to give us a new future. Paul would undoubtedly say our focus should be on looking forward as we cannot change the past. So far this is all about individual experience but there is bigger picture here.

As Christians we have been set free from our pasts while the world is captive to it. When we look at what is happening we see history repeating itself again and again. Ancient divisions remain despite all man's attempts to move on to a peaceful world. The United Nations endlessly debate and wrestle with intractable issues that have their roots in times long past. On every continent of the world there are historic ethnic tensions that repeatedly spill over into violence and war. The world is trapped in an endlessly repetitive back story. It cannot forget the past and there are many who want to keep reminding us of past atrocities and injustices. This has a major impact on fulfilling the great commission. Satan is acutely aware of this and exploits it because he knows that stirring up long standing animosities makes it harder to preach the gospel. He well knows what Jesus said: *'And this gospel of the kingdom will be preached in the whole world as a testimony to all nations, and then the end will come.' (Matthew 24 v 14)*. When the great commission has been fulfilled Satan knows he's finished so does everything he can to thwart the preaching of the gospel. He can't stop it but he can make it harder to do. That is what is behind all that is going in the world today. The world may be trapped in its endless back story but Jesus will come again to establish His Kingdom on earth and bring all things to a glorious conclusion.

The only back story worth remembering is *'For God so loved the world that He gave His one and only Son, that whoever believes in Him shall not perish but have eternal life' (John 3 v 16)*.

CHAPTER 27:

THE END OF DARKNESS

The Bible is very direct, it doesn't do fudge or vague. It means what it says because it is God's written word to us. Look at this verse: *'For he has rescued us from the dominion of darkness and brought us into the kingdom of the Son he loves' (Colossians 1 v 13)*. This says if you aren't in God's kingdom you are in darkness. Whatever we may think, without Jesus we are in the dark. We can't find our way through life and we can't see the true reality of creation. But there is a wonderful promise of light given around 700 years before Jesus was born. *The people walking in darkness have seen a great light; on those living in the land of the shadow of death a light has dawned' (Isaiah 9 v 2)*. This was a prophetic word about the Saviour to come and fulfilled at the birth of Jesus. See how the apostle John describes it: *'The true light that gives light to every man was coming into the world' (John 1 v 9)*. What this all adds up to is that without Jesus we remain in darkness or to put it bluntly, no Jesus means no light! Tragically this truth doesn't cause people to naturally seek Him who is the Light. See what Jesus Himself says: *This is the verdict: Light has come into the world, but men loved darkness instead of light because their deeds were evil' (John 3 v 19)*. Mankind's inherited sinful nature (why we sin) steers us towards darkness not light. What we need to understand is what holds us back from seeking the light when we see so much darkness in the world today.

There is a widespread desire for a more peaceful and better world. Sir Thomas More in 1516 wrote the book about Utopia, an imaginary idyllic society that has become the mantra for various movements for mankind to improve ourselves and lives. But the failure to produce a utopia by our own efforts has fuelled the opposite idea of a dystopian future for the world. Dystopia (based on the Greek words for bad or hard place) is defined as an imagined future state where there is suffering and injustice. In case you think this is some rarefied philosophical debate amongst academics you might be surprised at how far it has infused the modern world mind-set. There are a multitude of books, films and TV series that promote this fear of a bleak and hopeless future. A classic example is George Orwell's book 1984, Sci-Fi repeatedly uses this theme and cult TV series (e.g. The Prisoner) make this their storyline. Although these are all fiction they push the idea of a secretive malevolent power or elite controlling everyone and everything. But the endless reporting of scary world events moves dystopia from the realms of fiction into people's world view. Consider the main content of world news today: Climate change, terrorism, pandemics, oppressive regimes etc. This all develops a doom and gloom mind-set about the future, that we are to expect the worst. Dystopian propaganda is widespread today although people are unaware that they are sitting under it. This not only fosters a sense of hopelessness, but questions the existence of a loving God or, if He exists, is unwilling or incapable of helping us. This is why it is a serious obstacle to the gospel as it diverts people from seeking the only One who can save and change things. It is not difficult to see that this is exactly what Satan wants. He is opposed to love, hope, joy, freedom, fullness of life and instead promotes hate, despair, distress, oppression and a miserable existence. He wants to airbrush Jesus, salvation and redemption out of people's thinking to believe in a future without Christ.

But there is hope! There is no such thing as a future without the Lord Jesus Christ. He is coming back. The dystopian agenda blatantly ignores and denies the promise of His return when He will remove Satan from the scene and establish His 1,000 year reign on earth. When we will be able to enjoy His perfect justice, order and peace on earth before the end of time. Then there will be a new heaven and earth where we will be for eternity and *'There will be no more death or mourning or crying or pain, for the old order of things has passed away' (Revelation 21 v 4)*. This is God's answer to the false idea of a dystopian future for the world. He will bring an end to darkness. Furthermore, everyone is invited to enter this Kingdom of Heaven by embracing Jesus as the light of the world.

Now is our time for the church to shine the light of the gospel into our dark world. As is often said, the greater darkness the brighter the light shines! Jesus came into a dark world and He is going to come back again in brilliant glory. This is our message to the world: *When Jesus spoke again to the people, he said, "I am the light of the world. Whoever follows me will never walk in darkness, but have the light of life"* (John 8 v 12). So let the light shine through us today into the darkness of our world.

CHAPTER 28:
ANXIETY

You won't often find the word anxiety in the Bible but you increasingly find it in today's world, especially among young people. The media is reporting studies with school age children that reveal many are so pessimistic about not only their own futures but that the planet is doomed! And it is not only young people who think this as there is a growing sense of hopelessness about what lies ahead across all age groups. The fear of the unknown and calamity has exploded as a result of relentless exposure to news of pandemics, climate change together with endless arguments about whether anything can be done to avert disaster. Governments recognise that there is a mental health crisis looming and are scrambling to find answers. This is a crisis of the disappearance of hope. For many young people they see that their future is at best bleak or that it has been stolen. So are we doomed, is there any good news? What is needed now is hope, but not a naïve platitude that says 'don't worry everything will be OK'. Nor a vague wishy-washy idea that things will work out on their own. We need a definite and solid hope rooted in the promises of the Creator of the universe. Here is the good news: We have those promises despite what we see around us.

Let's begin with the hopeless situation that the people of Israel were in when they were taken into exile by the Babylonian empire. They had been uprooted from their homeland, lost their freedom and lived in an alien culture with no prospect of things turning around. But in the middle of all this hopelessness a young prophet called Jeremiah spoke these well-known words: '... *"For I know the plans I have for you," declares the LORD, "plans to prosper you and not to harm you, plans to give you hope and a future..."'* (*Jeremiah 29 v 11*). Here is God's promise to restore Israel and 70 years later it was fulfilled, they were able to return and re-establish themselves. Into their despair God injected the hope that all was not lost. As always, it is what

God says that counts not just what we see. What we see around us is the spur to seeking the God of the universe. At this point you might well say that was just for Israel and doesn't apply in our global situation. So let's look at an incident in Jesus' ministry.

A man had a son who was demon possessed. He couldn't speak, would suffer terrifying seizures and it seemed no-one could help. It was so severe that the demon would often throw the boy into a fire or water to kill him (see Mark 9 v 17 – 27). It was a hopeless situation with an awful future. When he is brought to Jesus the despairing father says: '... *if you can do anything, take pity on us and help us' (v 22)*. He had clearly heard about what Jesus could do but also had doubts about whether He would or could for his son. Listen to the reply: *"If you can?" said Jesus, "Everything is possible for him who believes." (v 23)*. Jesus' answer is an emphatic 'of course I can and will'. The father still struggling to believe says *"I do believe; help me overcome my unbelief" (v 24)*. The boy's father had faith and doubts all at the same time just like we do! And of course Jesus does deliver and fully restore the boy. In a totally hopeless situation He brings hope and a future back to life. Here we see that God's promise to give hope and a future is personal as well as for a nation. Now to this you might say that was then, what about now?

This incident teaches us that when we are in a hopeless situation we need to find Jesus. The story of the early Church contained in the Book of Acts is a record of successive deliverances from hopeless situations. After Jesus returned to heaven the disciples went out to preach the good news as they were told to do. Sins had been paid for in full by the sacrifice of Jesus on the cross and man could be at peace with God by receiving Him as their Saviour. But as the gospel went out, persecution increased and the church was under great pressure to stop telling the world about Jesus. Many times situations looked hopeless but the early Christians didn't give up because they knew something. Even if they perished they would immediately go to be with Jesus in heaven. Look at what Peter wrote: *'Praise be to the God and Father of our Lord Jesus Christ! In his great mercy he has given us new birth into a living hope through the resurrection of Jesus Christ from the dead...' (1 Peter 1 v 3)*. To the early church, Jesus was not dead but very much alive as a 'living hope'. When we believe in Jesus we are born again to a new life with a hope that is very much alive. It is not a hope that the world can give but a hope that is wrapped up in the person of Jesus. The apostle Paul put it like this: *To them God has chosen to make known among the Gentiles the glorious riches of this mystery, which is Christ in you, the hope of glory.' (Colossians 1 v 27).* In the gospel a mystery of God is revealed, which is that when you believe in Jesus He comes to live in you and He will never leave you. When you have Jesus in your life you have an indestructible hope in this life and in the life to come with Him in His glory.

The answer to this present crisis is the preaching of the gospel which has at its heart a powerful message of hope. When people of all ages have an encounter with Jesus they meet hope. When we have this hope, no matter how things pan out around us we will know that God has plans to give us hope and a future in this world and the next.

ABOUT THE AUTHOR

Chris Bomford lives in North Yorkshire with his wife Heather. They have been married for 50 years and have two grown up daughters and four grandchildren. They have both been involved in church leadership in Essex as pastors, inter-church initiatives and children's work. They were also involved in trips to Romania to deliver aid and preach in various churches.

Since moving to West Yorkshire in 2006 they have been involved with several different fellowships as they continue to hold to their desire to work with all denominations. Chris continued to carry out his itinerant preaching and Bible teaching work. A recent move to North Yorkshire has led them to The Hollybush Christian Fellowship near Thirsk, where they have now settled.

The consistent theme of all that they do is to see people come to a knowledge of the truth about Jesus along with a tangible experience of His love and power.